BIRTH OF THE CHURCH MATTHEW, MARK, LUKE, AND ACTS

Christian Living Bible Study Series

by Trina Bresser Matous

BIRTH OF THE CHURCH - MATTHEW, MARK, LUKE, AND ACTS BY TRINA BRESSER MATOUS
Published by Straight Street Books
an imprint of Lighthouse Publishing of the Carolinas
2333 Barton Oaks Dr., Raleigh, NC, 27614

ISBN: 978-1-946016-35-5

Cover design by writelydesigned.com
Interior design by Karthick Srinivasan

Available in print from your local bookstore, online, or from the publisher at: www.LPCbooks.com .

Follow the author online at: @TBresserMatous or facebook.com/TrinaWrites.

Brought to you by the creative team at LPCBooks.com: Eddie Jones, Shonda Whitworth, and Cindy Sproles.

Library of Congress Cataloging-in-Publication Data
Bresser Matous, Trina
Birth of the Church - Matthew, Mark, Luke, and Acts/Trina Bresser Matous 1st ed.
Printed in the United States of America

Praise for *Birth of the Church – Matthew, Mark, Luke and Acts*

It is hard to imagine anything more critical to a faithful walk with Jesus then a right understanding of the Word of God. Trina has done a great job creating a resource for anyone who wants to go deeper and understand more about the synoptic gospels and Acts. This in depth look at Matthew, Mark, and Luke and Acts, like all of Trina's work, is insightful, detailed, accurate, and accessible. It is written in a way that helps anyone who is interested in knowing more to understand. This book will be a great addition to anyone's study library.

~ **Douglas Kempton**
Senior Pastor Grace Community Church, Detroit

In a world where so many feel that truth is up for grabs, knowing God's word and its background is critical in helping us live lives that reflect His glory. Trina Bresser Matous does a phenomenal job of researching the background of the Bible and pulling out insights that are applicable to life. This volume would be a blessing for any who wants to not only know the Bible, but know how to apply the Bible to his or her life.

~ **Wayne Stapleton**
Pastor, Renewal Church

Trina Bresser Matous comes alongside us as a partner in discovering the transformational truth we each need to become more like Jesus. With well researched background information, concise overviews, relevant insights and questions that begged to be answered; Trina seems to be on a quest to equip every person to more thoroughly understand God's word and treasure it in their hearts.

~ **Norflette and Shenay Shumake**
Pastors, Life Changers International Ministries

Nearly a decade ago our church launched a comprehensive effort to encourage Bible reading in our congregation. In an effort to bring the readings to life, promote discussion and application within the body, Trina Bresser Matous invested full-time efforts reading ahead and creating overview notes of the upcoming weeks' readings. Her thorough research, summary and application notes were a huge catalyst to our body's daily engagement with the Scriptures. Over a number of years her work was updated and perfected. We are thrilled that this tool has now become bound in an easy to use series that can be enjoyed by the larger body of Christ. You will find using these supplements, in conjunction with your own Bible reading and study, an enormous encouragement.

~ **Bryce Gray Elder,**
Grace Community Church

Table Of Contents

MARK

LUKE

ACTS

Dedication

To the Posse

Dawn, Debby, Maureen, Peggy, Penny, and Victoria

You have been my encouragers, prayer warriors, and faithful friends.

We have shared many trials and joys and I can't imagine life without you.

Thank you for blessing me so abundantly!

Introduction

There are perhaps no more important words in the entire Bible than the words written about and spoken by Jesus. In one way or another, the whole of the Old Testament points forward to the coming Messiah, while Acts, the epistles and Revelation point back to Jesus as the promised Messiah. Understanding how the gospels present Jesus, what He did and said, and how those of His own time interacted with Him inform our understanding of the rest of the Bible.

Jesus' words give us an intimate look at God the Father and greater understanding of His plan for redeeming a people otherwise lost to the condemnation of sin. His words remind us that throughout human history, the God who loves us unconditionally and without reservation has pursued us. He has never been satisfied that the judgment for sin would forever separate us from Him. Instead, from the beginning of time, God had a plan that would allow for satisfaction of the judgment without the loss of relationship between Himself and us. And Jesus' words remind us that He made the ultimate, unselfish, and perfect sacrifice that we may enjoy a forever that never ends with the Creator and Lover of our souls. We have so much to gain by knowing Jesus through the gospels.

This third book in the Christian Living Bible Study Series includes the Synoptic Gospels—Matthew, Mark, and Luke—as well as Acts. The Greek word *synopsis* is the root of the word synoptic and means *a seeing together.*[1] These three gospels are called the Synoptic Gospels because of the similarity in their language, content, and arrangement.

Acts, also known as Acts of the Apostles, is the one historical book of the New Testament. It contains some of the events that took place following Jesus' resurrection and chronicles the growth and expansion of the early church following the ascension of Jesus.

These four books give invaluable information and wisdom for knowing and maturing in the Christian faith. In fact, without these

[1] R.F. Youngblood, *Nelson's New Illustrated Bible Dictionary* (Nashville: Thomas Nelson Publishers, 1995), 517

books, there would be a significant hole in our understanding of God and the relationship He calls us to. May your study be rich, insightful, and deeply satisfying.

How to use this book

The information given on the following pages should be read in conjunction with the Biblical text. I recommend you read the Biblical text first, then read the associated comments. As you do, ask the Holy Spirit for wisdom and insight.

I have attempted to make the information presented here non-translation specific. You may find, however, that a particular word being discussed does not appear in the translation you are using. The concept still applies. If you want to find the specific word being discussed, try looking at different translations, which are easily accessible online.

God's Word has many purposes. He uses it to communicate His great love for and mercy toward all of humanity. He also uses it to speak into our lives. For unbelievers, God uses His Word to drawn them into faith. For newer believers, He uses it to inform and grow their faith. For all believers, God uses His Word to mold and shape us more and more into the image of His Son. James reminded his readers that simply hearing God's Word was not enough; they needed to do it as well (Jam. 1.22). Questions at the end of each chapter are intended to be a catalyst for applying the Biblical text to our lives and experiences in the 21st century. I encourage you to seek and be open to the leading of the Holy Spirit. Spend time thinking about your responses, while being sensitive to promptings of the Holy Spirit to change attitudes, behaviors, or thought patterns.

Use in a small group setting

God uses other believers as well as His Word in our lives. Discussing the chapter-end questions in a small group setting can be beneficial. Other believers' viewpoints and insights can enhance our own understanding of the Biblical text in ways we may not gain on our own. They can also aid our understanding of and response to the trials, hardships, and difficulties we face in our lives. God tells us that we "sharpen" each other as we relate together over His word and what He is doing in our lives. (Prov. 27: 17)

God's Word is called the Living Word because God continually reveals new insights. Your insights from a passage may be different than a friend's. This is okay!

Don't be discouraged if your knowledge of the Bible and understanding of the text does not seem as comprehensive as someone else's. God is pleased with anyone who opens His Word and will reveal Himself through it.

Do be encouraged that as you continue to read, pieces will fit together, new understandings will surface, and revelations will emerge. Remember that God is gracious and merciful. He wants a relationship with you through His Son, Jesus Christ. So take a breath, enjoy His Word, and come to know Him better.

Enjoy your journey with God. His Word is rich and will add meaning to your life!

MATTHEW

The New Testament begins with the Gospel of Matthew, which is named after its author. Matthew, also known as Levi, was the Jewish tax collector Jesus called to be an apostle (Luke 5.27). As a tax collector, Matthew was despised by his countrymen. Yet after witnessing the power of the resurrected Christ, Matthew had a strong desire to share what he had learned with the people he knew were eagerly awaiting the coming Messiah.

Evidence of Matthew writing to his own people can be seen in the Jewish character of the gospel. For instance:

- Matthew assumed his readers understood Jewish customs and, therefore, did not explain them as did Mark.
- Matthew included a genealogy that showed Jesus descended from both Abraham (the father of the Jewish people) and David (from whom the Messiah was promised to descend). Son of David is used nine times in Matthew's gospel, more than the other three gospels combined.
- Matthew emphasized how Jesus fulfilled Old Testament prophecy more than any other gospel writer by referencing the Old Testament fifty-three times and alluding to it over seventy times.
- Matthew presented Jesus as the King the Jews had long awaited. Kingdom of heaven is used thirty-three times throughout the book.
- Jerusalem was referred to in distinctively Jewish terms—the holy city and city of the great King.

The Gospel of Matthew can be divided into four parts. The first, chapters 1-4, focuses on the announcement and birth of Jesus. Chapters 5-15 comprise the second part, which focuses on the message and teachings of Jesus. The third part, chapters 16-27, portrays Jesus' rejection and crucifixion while the final chapter conveys the resurrection of Jesus.

Matthew 1

BACKGROUND

In Jewish culture, genealogies were very important. They validated one's claim to be an Israelite, confirmed the tribe to which s/he belonged, and affirmed certain people's qualifications to serve in a priestly or Levitical position.

Betrothal was similar to modern day engagement, though much more binding and required a divorce to call off. Parents frequently arranged marriages, though with the consent of the bride and groom. The groom often paid a portion of the bride price during the betrothal, which usually lasted one year.

OVERVIEW

Though it was unusual for a Jewish genealogy to include women, Matthew included four in addition to Mary. Tamar had a child with her father-in-law (Gen. 38). Rahab was a Canaanite prostitute (Josh. 2). Ruth was a Moabite (Ruth 1.4). Bathsheba had an affair with David (2 Sam. 11-12). By including these women in the royal lineage, God shows His grace, His forgiveness of even the darkest of sins, that His plan for redemption extended beyond the nation of Israel, and that no one is beyond being used to bring about His plans.

The Old Testament includes a prophecy that the Messiah would descend from David (Jer. 23.5). Matthew's genealogy shows that Jesus fulfilled this prophecy.

Throughout the genealogy, Matthew used *begot* or *father of* to show the family line passing from father to son. In Greek, *of whom* is a singular feminine pronoun, indicating that Jesus was born of Mary. While not evident in English, the pronoun does not suggest or permit the inclusion of Joseph, thereby maintaining Jesus' conception through Mary and the Holy Spirit. Jesus physically descended from David through Mary, while legally descending from David through Joseph. In this way, David is established as one of Jesus' ancestors.

The name *Jesus* means "Yahweh is Savior" in Hebrew.

It is significant that God told Joseph what he was to name Mary's child. A father naming a baby indicated the father claimed the child as a member of the family. Thus God moved Joseph from rejecting Mary to adopting her child as his own.

Matthew's first mention of a fulfilled prophecy came from Isaiah 7.14, which pointed to the virgin birth of the promised Messiah.

Joseph was obedient to the message he received from God. He married Mary as he had planned but refrained from having sexual relations with Mary until after Jesus was born. Matthew's inclusion of the statement *did not know her* seems to indicate that Joseph and Mary had other children as later texts suggest (Matt. 13.55-56; Mk. 6.3). Some have suggested that Jesus' siblings were actually Joseph's children by a previous marriage. If that were true, however, Jesus would not have a legal claim to heir of David's throne since he would not have been Joseph's oldest son.

INSIGHTS

Both Mary and Joseph found themselves in difficult situations. Mary was pregnant by means she did not fully understand. Joseph was engaged to a woman who was carrying a child that was not his. Both faced grim futures. Joseph would have to divorce a woman he'd never married. Mary would have to raise a child without a husband or even risk death for apparently becoming pregnant outside marriage. When Joseph had his dream, he stood at a crossroads. He could believe, obey and participate in God's plan, or doubt and walk away. Our own choices can be just as difficult and the outcomes just as uncertain. We always do best when we choose to follow God, despite what unknowns loom ahead.

1. Forty-two generations covering hundreds of years are listed in verses 2-16, yet God remained true to His promise that Christ would come from Abraham's line. Do you believe God keeps His promises or do you doubt His abilities?

2. Joseph was able to put his trust in God after the Lord appeared to him in a dream. When God speaks to you, do you immediately trust as Joseph did or do you continue to question God's plans for you?

Matthew 2

BACKGROUND

Magi were astrologers who engaged in the practice of reading the stars. Those from the east, probably Persia, were particularly respected by the Greco-Roman world. If the magi were from Persia, they may have been exposed to the Jewish scriptures by the exiled Israelites when they were conquered by Babylon (which was later conquered by the Medo-Persians). Since Daniel had been a servant of the king in Babylon, his writings, which contain many Messianic prophecies, may still have been circulating.

Both Moses and Jesus were deliverers for people in bondage and both were threatened as infants.

OVERVIEW

The magi likely visited Jesus several months after His birth. Evidence for this includes Mary and Joseph living in a house by the time of the visit (2.11); Herod ordering the murder of all male children under the age of two (2.16), and Mary and Joseph making the ritual sacrifice for the poor (Lk. 2.22-24; Lev. 12.8), which would have been unnecessary if they had already received the magi's gifts.

The chief priests' answer to Herod's question (quoted from Mic. 5.2) is an indication of their familiarity with Messianic prophecy and the hope all Jewish people had in the coming Messiah.

Gold was a symbol of royalty. Frankincense, a fragrance, and myrrh, an ointment, were highly prized imports from the East.

Four times in this chapter, God used dreams to communicate His message: once to the magi (2.12) and three times to Joseph (with an additional time in the previous chapter; 1.20, 2.13, 19, 22).

The quote from Hosea (11.1) was originally written of the nation of Israel, who, as God's chosen or son, was brought out of Egypt. Jesus, as the Son of God, gave greater depth of meaning to the scripture.

The magi would have been traveling with a large entourage and would have been hard to miss as they traveled through the country. Their return would have naturally taken them through Jerusalem. When they did not appear, Herod would have known he had been deceived. The route to avoid Jerusalem likely took the magi south to Hebron, then west to Gaza before heading north along the rugged coastal road.

The prophecy predicting the slaughter of the Jewish children is found in Jeremiah 31.15. As with many prophecies, this one had both short and long-term fulfillments. Rachel, who had been buried near Bethlehem, was pictured as weeping when the Israelites were led into captivity in Babylon. The prophecy was also fulfilled by Herod's determined efforts to kill Jesus.

Archelaus, like Herod, had a reputation for being a cruel ruler. He survived for ten years before being deposed by the Romans following complaints by a Jewish delegation to Rome.

INSIGHTS

The precise nature of the magi's worship is unknown. They may have recognized Jesus as the person He was—Son of God. Or they may have recognized Him as an important God among many others. Likewise today, some mistakenly recognize Jesus only as a great prophet (Muslims) or a literal son of God without full equality (Jehovah Witnesses), or a host of other designations, but fail to recognize Him as the second Person of the triune God, whose death on the cross and resurrection from the dead provided the one perfect sacrifice that allowed humanity to be restored to relationship with God for all time.

1. The Magi were overjoyed when they saw the star that announced Christ's birth. They began a journey that eventually led to finding the Christ child in Bethlehem. Have you ever sought God and found Him (Proverbs 8:17)? Is there anything that is keeping you from seeking after God with your whole heart?

2. We see Joseph again spoken to in a dream and responding with immediate obedience. Do you listen for direction from God? Do you respond with immediate obedience when given direct instruction from God? If not, what prevents you from doing so?

Matthew 3

BACKGROUND

When a king planned to visit a particular area, preparations included repairing, leveling, and smoothing the road on which he would travel.

Pharisees and Sadducees were both religious leaders in the Jewish faith. The Pharisees adhered to the Law of Moses, the Prophets, and the Writings as well as oral traditions. The Sadducees were associated with the priests, focused on the temple, and followed only the Pentateuch (the first five books of both the Hebrew Scriptures and Old Testament).

OVERVIEW

John the Baptist served as Jesus' herald by announcing the imminent appearance of the Messiah. John's birth, ministry, and death all preceded those of Jesus. Unlike other prophets and religious leaders of the time who called for personal ceremonial cleansing, John baptized those who responded to his message of repentance.

By quoting the prophet's statement that the road be prepared for the return of the captives from exile, John was advocating the preparation of the nation's spiritual road in anticipation of the Messiah's arrival (Is. 40.3).

John's dress and diet were common to the very poor. It would have been unusual for a crowd to gather around a poor man. Rather it was John's message that caused people to gather.

It was a common belief of the Jewish people that one was saved simply by being Abraham's descendant. John challenged that idea by suggesting that God would clear the dead and unproductive "wood" out of the nation.

John recognized his role as herald by preaching repentance and baptizing the people while at the same time stating that one even greater than he was coming. Baptizing with the Holy Spirit began to occur on Pentecost and continues when each new believer receives the Holy Spirit. Baptizing with fire likely is a reference to God's coming judgment.

Jesus' desire to *fulfill all righteousness* was not a suggestion that He was baptized because He needed to repent. Rather, Jesus, who was without sin, confirmed John's ministry and fulfilled the will of His Father.

God's proclamation signaled the beginning of Jesus' ministry, confirmed Jesus as Messiah, and showed His pleasure in Jesus' obedience.

INSIGHTS

Jesus, of all people, did not need to be baptized. He was born and would live His entire life without sin. Yet in obedience to God's will, Jesus did what He did not need to do. God sometimes calls us to do things that appear to be meaningless to us. In our inability to see the bigger picture of God's sovereign plan, we may grumble at the inconvenience, embarrassment, or uncomfortableness of doing something we deem unnecessary. God is at work in ways we cannot completely comprehend and often uses these *meaningless* acts to test our obedience, bring glory to Himself, and draw those around us to the saving grace of His Son.

1. John the Baptist encouraged those who came to him to repent and turn back to God. Do you encourage those around you to turn their lives to God? Do you readily repent when you need to? What prevents you from doing so?

2. Jesus did not need to be baptized to prove who He was. He did it out of obedience to His Father's will. Sometimes God asks us to do things we may not understand. Will you respond in obedience, trusting in God's bigger plan?

Matthew 4

BACKGROUND

Galilee was an important region of the empire. The land was fertile and generally produced an abundant crop. Two trade routes also ran through it, which served as another means of fueling the local economy.

Fishing was an important part of the Galilean economy. Drying, salting, or pickling were the common means of preserving the fish. Fishermen generally made a better living than those who worked the land.

OVERVIEW

Jesus was led into the wilderness by the Holy Spirit, showing the dependency of one member of the Godhead upon another. Jesus' earthly ministry was accomplished with the help of the Holy Spirit's ministry.

Fasting is one means of setting aside one's own needs in order to focus on hearing from God. The Holy Spirit led Jesus to fast for forty days before beginning His earthly ministry in earnest.

Satan waited until Jesus was physically weak to tempt Him. The first two temptations questioned Jesus' position and authority as the Son of God (*if* you are), while the third temptation attempted to replace Jesus with Satan.

Jesus responded to each temptation by quoting scripture. In response to the first temptation, Jesus quoted Deuteronomy 8.3. It was not morally wrong to turn stones into bread, but doing so was outside of God's will. Jesus did not need to prove Himself, but He did need to remain obedient to the Father.

Satan attempted to use scripture himself in the second temptation (Ps. 91.11-12), but he used it out of context and twisted it for his own purposes. In response, Jesus quoted Deuteronomy 6.16, which warns against tempting God.

In the final temptation, Satan attempted to give Jesus a crown that did not require a cross. The only crown of any real value would come after Jesus had suffered on the cross in obedience to His Father. Jesus responded by quoting Deuteronomy 6.13, the commandment stipulating that only God is to be worshipped.

Isaiah foretold of the Jesus' ministry, not only in the Galilean region but to the Gentiles as well (Is. 9.1-2).

Jesus' appeal to repent was the same as John the Baptist's (3.2).

Normally, people choose to become students of a rabbi, rather than the rabbi choosing his students.

Matthew may have mentioned Syria because it had a large Jewish population.

INSIGHTS

As Jesus called the disciples, they responded in obedience and followed Him, often leaving lucrative occupations. It is likely that all had previously heard about Jesus before He called them. It is interesting to note that those Jesus called were ordinary men; none came from either political or religious positions of power. Many times we can be tempted to respond to God's call by thinking we don't know enough, we're not well placed enough, or we're not influential enough. Just as Jesus did with those He called, God will prepare us for what He calls us to before sending us out. Our obedience is of greatest value to God.

1. Jesus refutes all of Satan's temptations with the Word of God. Do you use God's Word to fight off temptation? Find a verse that is personal for your situation and use it to remind you of the power of God over your life every time you feel tempted.

2. Matthew ties Jesus to the ancient prophecy of Isaiah to prove His Lordship. Do you believe Jesus is the Messiah who came to fulfill God's promise?

3. In this chapter Jesus calls the first four disciples. They were just ordinary fisherman who responded in obedience. Scripture says they immediately left their work and followed. When Jesus calls you to follow Him, do you immediately change course, trusting God's power in you, or do you doubt your ability as an ordinary follower?

Matthew 5

BACKGROUND

Chapters 5-7 are known as the Sermon on the Mount. Matthew appears to have recorded a more comprehensive account of a sermon that was likely given on several occasions than was recorded by Luke (Luke 6). The Sermon's intent was not to present the way to salvation. Rather, it gave instruction on how to live righteously once the people had responded to Jesus' invitation to repent (4.17).

OVERVIEW

For rabbis, it was customary to stand to read scripture and sit to expound on it or teach. Often the rabbi's disciples would sit at his feet. Jesus' disciples were not limited to the apostles, whom He chose for special instruction.

Verses 3-12 are called the Beatitudes, from a Latin word meaning *blessed*. Each beatitude is comprised of three parts: a blessing, a condition of life, and the reason for feeling blessed. Jesus did not describe different types of people through the beatitudes. Rather, he was pointing to qualities those who inherited the kingdom would possess.

The four verses following the beatitudes have often been called similitudes. The beatitudes focused on *being* while the similitudes shifted the focus to *doing*.

Jesus' teachings caused some to question whether He intended to invalidate the law. Jesus affirmed the role of the law and that He would serve as the fulfillment of the law.

A jot is the smallest letter in the Hebrew alphabet while a tittle refers to a tiny distinguishing mark at the end of another Hebrew letter. Jesus' use of these terms in His statement about the law provides one of the strongest Biblical assertions regarding the inerrancy of scripture.

The *righteousness of the scribes and Pharisees* was external and activity oriented. They were viewed as far above the ordinary person in religious matters. To hear that more than what these men did was required would have been discouraging. Jesus later made clear that it was not works that gained one entrance into heaven, but faith in Him.

Beginning with verse 21 and continuing through the end of the chapter, Jesus contrasted the law with genuine Godly character, also called attitude of the heart. In each case, Jesus extended the law to include greater depth of meaning, thereby raising the standard of what was necessary to adhere to the commandment. These contrasts pointed to the ability to keep the law while remaining far from embodying the Godly character or heart God desires. Each comparison begins with *you have heard* or *it has been said*. While some of these statements were outlined in the Old Testament, Jesus was looking at the interpretation promoted by many rabbis and teachers. It was this interpretation, not the Old Testament teachings Jesus was questioning. The contrasting statement is introduced by *but I say to you* or *but I tell you*. Summary of the contrasts:

- Murder included anger
- Adultery included lust (mental adultery)
- Divorce included causing another to sin
- Swearing falsely was extended to not swearing at all
- Revenge was turned into forgiveness
- Hating one's enemies became loving one's enemies.

Raca is an Aramaic word meaning "empty headed."

INSIGHTS

Jesus did not forbid taking solemn oaths such as those to tell the truth in a court of law or to remain faithful to one's spouse in a marriage ceremony. He was condemning those that were a part of a person's common speech; those that suggest what s/he says cannot be trusted. Such oaths are popular today and are often introduced by, "I swear," "I swear to/by God," "As God is my witness," "By God," etc. Oaths made without careful thought have a tendency to compromise the oath-taker's integrity because they are often not said seriously or are not kept. They also dishonor God by using His name in a frivolous, disrespectful way.

1. This chapter contains a section of scripture often called the beatitudes. Jesus encouraged His listeners to adopt these attitudes of the heart as their own. These characteristics of humility, meekness, righteousness, mercy, etc. are not natural for us. Are you willing to let Jesus change your heart and attitudes into His so that you can receive His kingdom blessings?

2. Jesus' message in this chapter contradicted in many ways the traditions the Jewish people believed and held to be true. Are you willing to search God's Word to find His Truth for your life's circumstances and not rely on your own thoughts and ideas?

Matthew 6

BACKGROUND

Jesus taught his disciples not to *pray … as the heathen* (pagans) *do.* Greeks and Romans often used as many names and titles as possible when they prayed to their deities. They also continually reminded the deities of any sacrifices they had made in worship. In this manner, they hoped to invoke the favor of the deity that they might enjoy the blessings of life rather than the curses.

OVERVIEW

Jesus taught that people should not be concerned about what other people thought of them, but rather what God thought. He addressed three instances in which it was easy to be motivated by the praises of men: charitable deeds, praying, and fasting.

The Greek verb in *have their reward* was a legal term meaning "paid in full." Those who did their deeds of charity for all to see would be paid in full through the compliments they received from those around them. On the other hand, God Himself would reward those who did not seek approval and accolades for their deeds.

Jesus did not condemn praying in public. Rather, just as with charity, He was questioning the motive upon which one acted. Neither did Jesus condemn long prayers; instead, he was referring to the empty repetition of words. Prayer should reflect a sincere desire of the heart to communicate with God, not a mindless, ritualistic activity that required little thought.

Jesus' statement to *pray in this way* did not mean exactly the following words had to be used. Though there is nothing wrong with repeating the words of the Lord's Prayer, they can become the empty recitation Jesus warned against.

The Lord's Prayer contains six requests; the first three seek the kingdom to come, while the second three ask God to fulfill the needs of His people in the meantime.

Fasting done according to Jewish ritual included abstinence from pleasures as well as food. Pharisees took this even farther by wearing mourning garb and looking disheveled.

Treasures on earth are material goods such as money, houses, cars, etc. Treasures in heaven are rewards for faithful service. Jesus did not prohibit one from having material goods, but excess accumulation of goods was an indication that one's heart was not focused on achieving God's will.

Mammon is an Aramaic word meaning money or possessions. Two masters cannot be served because at some point, they will make conflicting demands.

Jesus moved from the danger of having a great many possessions to the danger of having too few—worry. Worry is unnecessary because God takes care of the needs of His people even more than He does those of the birds and flowers, for which He fully provides. It is also unnecessary because it cannot change anything as Jesus pointed out when He asked if worry could change one's stature. One's ability not to worry comes from his/her inner connection with God rather than from outward appearances.

Both greed and worry have their answer in God. Seeking His will and His ways first will set everything else in order, with God providing for all that is needed.

INSIGHTS

Some people have wondered about the necessity of praying if *your Father knows the things you have need of before you ask Him* (v. 8). The purpose of prayer is not to try to change God's will. Rather, it is about conforming our will to His. Through prayer, we seek to know the heart of God and to do His will. Although He already knows our needs, bringing them to Him is a means of expressing our trust and confidence in His plans and purpose for our lives and the lives of those around us.

1. Verse 2 says when you give to the needy … indicating an expectation from God. How are you at giving to those in need around you and worldwide?

2. Jesus instructs us to make prayer and fasting private activities between God and us alone, not something for public display. How does it make you feel to know God wants a private, personal relationship of intimacy between Him and you?

3. Worry is something that plagues most of us. How do Jesus' words not to worry challenge you to trust Him with your life?

Matthew 7

BACKGROUND

False prophets were not new to Jesus' time. God had warned His people against false teachings since the time of Moses. False prophets were those who led people away from God rather than to Him. Such leading could come in a variety of forms, including teachings, dreams, signs, and wonders. Prophets were to be judged by what they said, particularly when they forecasted future events. If the events did not come to pass, they were to be judged as false and stoned to death (Deut. 13.1-5; 18.20-22).

OVERVIEW

Jesus did not forbid judgment. Rather, He was stating that the standards used to judge another would be used on the one judging, i.e. judging justly, rashly, vengefully, etc.

Dogs and pigs were both considered unclean; dogs because they were scavengers and pigs because they would eat anything, including the foulest of foods. Multiple meanings are possible for the proverb including giving correction only to those who will listen or giving only to those who want what is given.

Jesus used the words *ask, seek,* and *knock* in the present tense, suggesting a frequent and persistent approach to prayer. Jesus followed the instruction with two examples of a father providing for his son and both requests, bread and fish, were basic staples for the people Jesus taught. While God will provide, there is no suggestion in Jesus' words that God would grant *whatever* one asked for.

The final section of the Sermon on the Mount presents a series of contrasts that serve to illustrate the choice each listener has to make. The contrasts are: two ways, two trees, two professions, and two foundations. Such contrasts were a common teaching method for both Jews and Greeks.

Most Jews believed simply being a part of Israel would save them. Those who would not be saved would be a few exceptions. Jesus, however, taught the opposite. The few who would be saved would not be saved because they were a part of the Israelite nation but rather because they chose the right path—believing in Jesus.

Thorn bushes and thistles were common weeds that grew among crops. They were worthless and made harvesting difficult.

The *fruit* of false prophets was not only what they did, but also what they taught. False prophets were to be judged by the results of their words. The scriptures provide a base against which what they taught could also be judged.

Jesus stated the most important thing was to do the will of God. He implied that it was possible to perform miracles, yet not be doing so in accordance with God's will. Therefore, a person's words and actions need to align themselves with God and His purposes in order to be judged righteous.

The key to the last contrast is not appearance, but foundation. Nothing is said of the two houses' appearance. What made the difference in their ability to withstand the elements of nature was the foundation on which they were built. Likewise, the person who built his/her life on the foundation of right relationship with Christ would withstand His judgment. Those who built their lives on anything else were like the house on sand and would fail the coming test.

INSIGHTS

Jesus used a series of contrasts to illustrate the choice each person must make, a choice between accepting Jesus for who He said He is and rejecting His claim. While many today want to believe there are many ways to get to heaven, the Christian scriptures repeatedly and clearly state that the only way to enjoy heaven is through faith in Christ. This may seem unfair and out of the realm of what a loving God would do, however, it is within the bounds of what a just God would do. God cannot be loving without also being just. We can decide what we would like to be true, but this does not change what God has stated *is* true.

1. Jesus instructs us to be aware of the people around us. We are to pay attention to the fruit they produce by the behaviors they choose to engage in. Do you obey Jesus' instruction to choose your friends carefully, making wise choices for yourself?

2. Matthew relays that the crowds were amazed at Jesus' teaching! Does God's word amaze you? If not, ask Him to wow you today with insight only He can give to you.

Matthew 8

BACKGROUND

One of the most important duties of an eldest son was burying his parents upon their death. Failure to do so would have been to dishonor one's parents. Two burials took place. The first was immediately after death and included preparing and anointing the body. The second took place a year later. Once the flesh had rotted off the bones, the bones were gathered up, placed in a box and buried in a slot in the tomb. This minimized the overall space needed by making the tomb available for additional burials.

OVERVIEW

The leper's request for healing *if you are willing* was a display of the leper's faith rather than a question of the Lord's ability to perform. From the leper's perspective, if healing did not take place it was because Jesus chose not to, not because He did not have the ability to do so.

Ceremonial uncleanness was transferred from those who were unclean to those who were clean through touch or other contact. Here Jesus worked in reverse. By touching the leper, Jesus did not become unclean but caused the leper to become clean.

Jesus respected the Law of Moses by instructing the leper to present himself before the priests with the expected sacrifice (Lev. 14.1-32).

Only twice is Jesus said to marvel, once in response to the centurion's understanding of authority and the other as a reaction to the unbelief of His own townspeople (Mark 6.6).

The Jewish people believed they were God's called people and sitting with the great patriarchs of the faith (Abraham, Isaac, and Jacob) was their hope for the future, though not a hope for the Gentiles. That the Gentiles would sit with the patriarchs and the *sons of the kingdom*, the Jewish people, would be cast into *outer darkness* would have been a shocking thought for the people of Jesus' time.

Matthew quoted Isaiah 53.4 indicating that healing the multitudes was further fulfillment of the messianic prophecies.

Jesus' comment to let the *dead bury the dead* was directed toward properly ordering one's priorities, not toward dishonoring one's parents.

Jesus rebuked the disciples for their little faith because they had repeatedly seen Him work miracles, yet had not gained full understanding of who He was.

Several things about demons are revealed in Jesus' interaction with them: they recognize the deity of Jesus, they know they will be judged (before the time is a reference to the final judgment); and they recognize the authority of Jesus over their actions.

For the Jewish mindset, pigs would have been an appropriate place for the demons to go. It is likely that those watching would have believed the demons suffered the same fate as the pigs.

INSIGHTS

Since touching anything that was unclean resulted in ceremonial uncleanness, lepers were avoided and even shunned. Jesus' willingness to touch the leper demonstrated His greater concern for people's needs than for ceremonial ritual. Today, we may often find ourselves drawing away from and even repulsed by those who don't meet a particular set of standards. At those moments, it is worth asking ourselves some questions.

- Am I showing the love of Christ in how I interact with a particular person?
- Am I putting anything above Christ's command to minister to the lost?
- Am I willing to risk whatever is necessary to follow Christ wherever He leads?

1. Jesus had compassion toward those who were suffering and healed many of the physical disease and demon possession they suffered from. The common thread among these people was the faith each had that Jesus could heal them. What do you believe about Jesus' power and ability to heal our physical bodies today? If you or someone you know suffers from a physical ailment that has not been healed after asking Jesus to do so, how has your faith been affected?

2. When Jesus calmed the seas, He showed His power was not limited to physical healing but extends over nature as well. What do you believe about Jesus' power over nature? Do you think there is any limit to what Jesus can do?

Matthew 9

BACKGROUND

Chapters 8 and 9 contain a series of ten miracles told in nine stories. Matthew begins with three miracles (8.1-17), then moves to teaching (8.18-22). Three more miracles (8.23-9.8) are then followed by more teaching (9.9-17). The final three stories (9.18-33) include one story with two miracles. These miracles serve as a confirmation of Jesus' message in the Sermon on the Mount. The mandates about kingdom living are backed up by a display of the King's power and prove His ability to deliver what He promised.

OVERVIEW

Their faith refers to the faith of the paralytic as well as the faith of the men willing to bring their friend to Jesus.

Blasphemy was committed when God's name was used in a dishonoring way. The scribes' accusation that Jesus was blaspheming was false. They may have extended the definition to include doing or attempting to do what only God could do.

Forgiving sins was easier because there was no proof that it had occurred. No one could deny that the harder healing had taken place when the man was able to get up and walk.

Pharisees were particular about their eating rules and avoided eating with those who did not observe the same rules. Believing Jesus to be a wise teacher, they thought He would share their beliefs. When He did not, they expressed their amazement and questioned whether He really was wise.

When Jesus called the Pharisees righteous, He was referring to their view of themselves rather than God's view of them. (No one is righteous before God apart from faith in Christ.) Jesus affirmed God's desire for relationship with His people rather than ritual sacrifice and other pious displays by quoting Hosea 6.6.

The Law required fasting only on the Day of Atonement. Pharisees often practiced it twice a week. Since it was often practiced with prayer and repentance, most rabbis and their followers engaged in the practice more than the once a year requirement. Jesus did not condemn the practice of fasting. Rather, He suggested His disciples should take advantage of His presence with them while they could since there would come a day when He would no longer be with them.

Wine was often stored in animal skins, which would stretch as the wine fermented. Putting new wine into old containers risked rupturing the already stretched out skin as the newer wine expanded.

Falling at the feet was an act of adoration or worship reserved for those of much greater status. Falling at Jesus' feet would have been unexpected and served as a means of recognizing Jesus' power and authority.

A continual flow of blood would have rendered a woman constantly unclean, creating a social and religious problem as well as a physical one.

By acknowledging the unclean woman who touched Him in the eyes of the crowd, Jesus made Himself ceremonial unclean. Again, He offered compassion to the marginalized and extended *cleanness* (healing) where uncleanness had previously prevailed.

Jesus' primary purpose was to bring spiritual healing to the people. By instructing the blind man not to tell anyone how he had been healed, Jesus attempted to minimize the number of people who heard about the miracle and thereby seek only physical healing for themselves.

Because the Pharisees could not deny the miracles Jesus performed, they attributed them to Satan.

INSIGHTS

Jesus' compassion on the people because they were without a shepherd was a strong indictment against the religious leaders of the day. Though very religious, they did not provide the spiritual leadership to which God had called them. Today we can fall into the same trap by appearing religious but not providing the spiritual leadership God would have us give. All of us are called to provide some type of leadership, be it to a spouse, congregation, offspring, co-worker, friend, acquaintance, or even a stranger. The compassion Jesus' felt should motivate us to fill, even in a small way, the need that is all around us.

1. Jesus worked tirelessly to help those around Him who were lost. Are you aware of those around you who need Jesus in their lives? How can you share Jesus' love, grace, and mercy with those who are lost?

2. The Pharisees were constantly trying to defeat Jesus and His disciples. Yet Jesus was not afraid and continued with the work God had sent Him to do. Do you press forward in your faith walk despite those who may take offense to your faith?

Matthew 10

BACKGROUND

In the gospel accounts, the term *Son of Man* was used only by Jesus and only to describe Himself. Though Jesus will eventually come to reign, the term describes the way in which Jesus initially came to earth: as a man to serve humanity. His death on the cross defeated sin, thereby setting the foundation for His return and reign over all the earth.

OVERVIEW

The twelve were initially called disciples, which emphasized the learning one did as they followed a rabbi. When the twelve were named, Matthew used the word *apostle,* which means "sent ones" and emphasized the authority they had been given by their master.

Three of the four gospel writers include a list of the names of the apostles (Matt. 10.2-4; Mark 3.16-19; Luke 6.14-16). The names in all three are the same save one. Mark and Matthew refer to *Thaddeus,* while Luke refers to *Judas, son of James.* Ancient documents indicate it was common practice for people to go by more than one name. As a result, it is thought that the two different names, usually a Greek or Roman name along with a Hebrew one, refer to the same person.

While some may have interpreted the *lost sheep of Israel* as the ten lost tribes, it is more likely Jesus used the reference in the Old Testament sense: people who had strayed from God.

Jesus sent the apostles out to continue the work He was doing. His instructions to take nothing would have caused the apostles to be totally focused on the work and not distracted by possessions they might have otherwise taken. It also caused them to be dependent on the provision and generosity of others.

Peace was as much a prayer for blessing as it was a greeting.

The serpent was viewed as cunning and therefore its wisdom worth imitating.

Jesus warned His followers that carrying His message as He instructed would be met with resistance and persecution. Despite whatever came, they were to rely upon the revelation and empowerment of the Holy Spirit. They would be persecuted just as Jesus Himself would suffer persecution.

Baal was a Canaanite deity. It is thought that the Jews may have added *zebub*, meaning "lord of the flies", to the name as a way of mocking the pagan god.

The only one able to destroy both body and soul is God. Though Satan may try and even succeed in destroying the body, he cannot destroy the soul. Therefore, God is the one to be feared.

Just as fear of God is rightly placed, so is trust in Him. Although He is the ruler of the entire universe, He is also aware of and cares about the minutest of details.

Jesus recognized that following Him had its cost. He promised, however, that those who acknowledged Him as Lord would be acknowledged before God. In other words, those willing to pay the cost would be rewarded.

In the last several verses of this chapter, Jesus focuses on doing those things that will bring an eternal reward. He does not want anyone to miss out on their future reward because of wrong attitudes they have in the present.

INSIGHTS

God is a God of details who does not miss even a cup of water given in His name. People may be tempted to think that God is impersonal and uncaring; that He set the universe in motion and has had little concern thereafter about what happens. The opposite is true. God does care and often shows Himself in the smallest of details. He is not a puppet who responds to our every desire or a genie that grants our every request. Instead, God is the mighty ruler of the universe whose main concern is for all humanity to enjoy the salvation He offers and know Him personally and intimately. Everything He does works toward that end.

1. Jesus did not promise the disciples easy lives, yet they were still willing to sacrifice their comfort and follow Him. How would you rate your willingness to be His follower in spite of the discomfort that comes with it? Is there anything you need to lay aside in order to follow Jesus more wholeheartedly? If so, how will you go about doing so?

2. Jesus states that He did not come to bring peace but a sword. The freedom and redemption from sin that Jesus offers results in changes to the ways we think and behave. These changes sometimes result in division within our families and with our friends. How does that make you feel? Do you pray that Jesus will be working in the midst of the division?

Matthew 11

BACKGROUND

Capernaum served as a base of operations for Jesus' ministry. It was located on the Sea of Galilee's north shore. Chorazin was two and a half miles north of Capernaum while Bethsaida was three miles east. Tyre and Sidon were pagan cities not highly thought of by Jews. The apparent willingness of some pagans to repent when they heard the truth of God's Word is reminiscent of Nineveh in the book of Jonah.

OVERVIEW

Although John was certain of God's call on him to proclaim the coming and appearance of the Messiah, it seems he was less certain about how the Messiah would appear. John may have expected that the Messiah would immediately establish His kingdom and judge Israel, as was commonly believed at the time. In response to John's question, Jesus quoted an Old Testament prophecy that stated the Messiah would perform miracles of healing (Is. 35.5-6).

A reed was a tall, slender, fragile plant in the grass family. It would easily bend and break in the wind, so was viewed as weak and unreliable.

Jesus quoted another Old Testament prophecy to show that the promised forerunner to the Messiah had been fulfilled (Mic. 3.1).

A very Jewish form of praise was to call someone the *greatest* as Jesus did John. Stating that the least in the kingdom was greater than John was a means of elevating the others, not diminishing John.

Malachi 4.5 promises the return of Elijah. The people of John's day expected Elijah to return as the Messiah established His kingdom. Jesus may have been indicating that John came in the spirit and power of Elijah.

Jesus used children pretending to have weddings or funerals as an analogy for the dissatisfaction John and Jesus' opponents felt toward them. These opponents were not pleased no matter how John and Jesus presented themselves.

Throughout scripture, God has favored the lowly and given little credence to those who boast in their own ability and wisdom (Ps. 138.6; Prov. 16.19).

Jesus recognized the burden religious regulations promoted by the priests, Pharisees, and other leaders created for the people. He offered an alternative that would give them relief from such a weighty load.

INSIGHTS

Some have wondered if *more tolerable for Sodom ... than for you* means that judgment on some will be easier than judgment on others. God's Word indicates that all sin is equal in His eyes because it is punishable by death. Yet it may be that God will show greater mercy toward the ignorant than to those who have heard and understood His Word. However God judges, He is trustworthy and His judgment is just. We can also rest assured that we will be judged based on our own degree of obedience as it compares to God's Word and call on our lives, *not* in comparison to how others have responded to God.

1. In the desert during his ministry, John the Baptist was confident about who Jesus was and the calling he had been given to proclaim Jesus' coming. When John was imprisoned and cut off from his followers, he began to question his beliefs about Jesus. Jesus, in His kindness and compassion, reassured John that He really was Messiah and that all John had preached was true. He encouraged John by calling him the greatest born of women. Are you willing to be honest with Jesus about your uncertainties and doubts? Do you allow Jesus to come in kindness, compassion, and with encouragement when you are questioning your faith and beliefs? He will meet and reassure you too!

2. Jesus invites us to, "Come to me, all you who are weary and burdened, and I will give you rest." (v. 28) In what ways do you accept His invitation to give your weary and burdened heart to Him and receive His rest?

Matthew 12

BACKGROUND

The Queen of Sheba lived during the time of Solomon. Prompted by rumors of Solomon's great wisdom and wealth she traveled to Israel to find out if the rumors were true. After questioning Solomon, the Queen discovered he was even more wise and prosperous than the rumors had stated (1 Kin. 10.1-13). While the actual location of Sheba is unknown, it is believed to have been in the Arabian Peninsula, in what is modern day Yemen.

OVERVIEW

For the Pharisees and scribes, the Sabbath was representative of the whole Law of Moses. From their perspective, disregarding the Sabbath was akin to disobeying the entire Law. Technically, the disciples were picking grain to eat and not for purposes of profit, so were not actually breaking the Law. The Pharisees, wanting to show Jesus was a lawbreaker, were trying to argue that the disciples were *reaping* rather than filling a personal need. They also interpreted healing as work rather than mercy toward another.

As *Lord of the Sabbath,* Jesus was qualified to say what honored God and what did not.

From this point forward in Matthew, opposition to Jesus' ministry continues to increase and culminates in His arrest and execution.

Matthew quoted one of the *Servant Songs* in Isaiah (42.1-4), which in context, called Israel to testify to God's glory. It also hinted that an individual would ultimately glorify God when Israel failed to do so. In addition, the passage made clear that Jewish opposition would lead to Gentile blessing.

The Pharisees' attempt to explain Jesus' power to heal was negated by three arguments set forth by Jesus. First, anything that attacks itself (i.e. is divided) cannot continue to exist. Second, the Pharisees claimed power given by God when their own followers did the same things Jesus did. Third, Jesus, as Messiah, had the ability to overcome the strongest opposition, an indication that the hoped for kingdom was near.

Blasphemy against the Spirit is thought by many to be the permanent rejection of Christ's identity and the saving power that comes through Him. Such revelation comes through the Holy Spirit. Therefore, rejecting Christ is also a rejection of the revelation given by the Holy Spirit. Note that "blasphemy" occurs with the *permanent* rejection of Christ, not a rejection that later turns to acceptance.

Just as a tree is judged good or bad by the quality of the fruit it produces, so the same applies to humans. What they produce through their actions will provide one means of determining the nature of a person's heart. In the case of the Pharisees, they continually asked Jesus to justify Himself by posing questions that were designed to trap Him. In the process of doing so, they overlooked the clear evidence provided by His ability to do miracles.

The people of Nineveh responded to Jonah's message. The Ninevites would be among those who would judge the Pharisees because they did not respond to the message of the One who brought greater freedom and judgment than Jonah.

Jesus' ability to cast out demons was not met with a real desire to reform. As a result, greater hardness of heart settled on Israel than they had had previously.

INSIGHTS

God will often respond to genuine requests for signs when He knows the motivation of the requester is to increase his/her faith. The Pharisees' request was not motivated by such a desire. They had already determined what they thought was true and would not allow evidence to the contrary to sway them. As a result, Jesus called them *evil and adulterous*. Our motivation in asking for a sign from God should come from a genuine motivation to grow in our own faith in Christ. Any other motivation is an attempt to manipulate God. Just as He did with the Pharisees, such requests will be recognized for what they are and condemned.

1. The Pharisees were caught up in their self-imposed laws about the Sabbath. Jesus tried to change their hearts and teach them that He desired to show mercy to His people no matter the day. What rules, if any, do you live by that are either self-imposed or imposed by others and not from God? What is the truth God wants you to know in place of these rules?

2. Jesus spoke about the importance of the words that we choose to speak. Are you aware of how and what you speak to those around you? When do you have a tendency to be careless with your words? How can you be more Christ-like in what you say?

3. When the people wanted a sign to be convinced of Jesus' identity, He pointed to the signs they were already familiar with: the people of Nineveh who repented when they heard Jonah's message and the Queen of the South who sought out Solomon's wisdom. Where is your heart? Do you believe Jesus is who He said He is—the Son of God? Take a moment to ask God to reveal any lies you believe about Him and replace those lies with His truth.

Matthew 13

BACKGROUND

Chapters 12 and 13 mark a turning point in Jesus' ministry and teaching. Chapter 12 focused on the Pharisees' and other religious leaders' rejection and failure to see how Jesus' ministry and message fulfilled the Old Testament messianic prophecies. In Chapter 13, Jesus focused on training His apostles and the multitudes who followed Him in the truth the religious leaders rejected.

Parables, Jesus' preferred method of teaching, generally contained one basic truth that was often bolstered by several points in the story.

OVERVIEW

Palestine has quite a bit of rocky land that is covered by only a thin layer of soil. Farmers sometimes sowed seed on land that had not been plowed first. As a result, they could never be sure whether they were sowing seed on ground that would sustain good crop growth.

No farmer would have evenly distributed seed on the four different soil types mentioned. Therefore, the parable should not be taken to indicate that only a quarter of all who hear the message of Christ will receive it. Rather, it should be interpreted as representative of the different ways people who hear Christ's message may respond.

The three soils in which the seed did not grow or grow well represent different ways a person might respond to the message they hear. They may be unwilling to turn from their sinful ways, may cave to outside persecution and peer pressure, or may be more attracted to the world's pleasures. Only those who trust in God's Word and nurture His truth will experience the fruit of God in their lives.

Jesus often began His parables by stating, "x is like y" (for instance, *the kingdom of heaven is like a man …*). Jesus intended that the subject (the kingdom) be explained by the whole parable, not just by the word that followed "like" (the man). These parables aimed at revealing a new truth about the subject rather than reveal the entire truth.

Tares were a poisonous weed that closely resembled wheat. It could only be distinguished once the ear (fruit) appeared. Farmers would let both grow until just prior to the wheat harvest when the tares would be weeded out. Likewise, believers and nonbelievers will be allowed to remain together until the final judgment.

While not the smallest known seed of the times, the mustard seed was very small for the large plant it produced. The point of the parable is that the kingdom would start in obscurity but expand to include all that was promised.

The parables about the lost treasure and the pearl of great price (found only in Matthew) are directed toward believers. The kingdom to come is worth far more than anything on earth; any sacrifice or inconvenience is not too great. The parable does not mean that all one possessed had to be sacrificed in order to be granted salvation. Rather, it meant that serving God's kingdom was to be the highest priority.

The disciples were sent out to gather as many as they could to the kingdom. It was not their responsibility to determine who should gain entrance. The angels would do that.

New and old treasures referred to the old truths found in the Old Testament and the new truths Jesus was revealing.

Nazareth was a small town of 1,500-2,000 inhabitants. Jesus would have been familiar to many who could not get past where He came from in order to see who He was.

INSIGHTS

While many think it is unfair of God to give more to those who already have and take away from those who do not have, there is a greater principle at work than equal distribution of wealth. Because God created everything, everything belongs to Him. He has given parts of His creation to humans to steward for Him. Those who steward well will be given the responsibility of caring for more, while those who are careless or selfish in their stewarding duties will lose what they have. Just as a wealthy man pays attention to how those who work for him care for his possessions and reward them accordingly, so God does with all of creation.

1. This chapter begins with the parable of the sower, which Jesus then interprets. It contrasts four different responses to God's Word that are generally applied to how people respond to the gospel, though it can also be applied to the condition of our hearts. Where is your heart right now? What areas of your heart need an overhaul and to be filled with good soil ready to grow the seed God plants there?

2. Jesus tells two parables about the separation of the good from the evil. What do you believe about God and His justice? Do you think the evil of this world will one day be destroyed? Why or why not?

Matthew 14

BACKGROUND

The Herod here is Antipas, Herod the Great's son. Herod the Great died a few years after Jesus' birth. His kingdom was divided between three sons, Antipas, Philip, and Archelaus. Tetrarch originally meant ruler of a quarter of some territory. Roman authorities later applied it to a ruler of any portion of land.

Feeding the five thousand is the only pre-crucifixion miracle recorded in all four gospels.

OVERVIEW

John the Baptist had condemned Herod when Herod divorced his wife in order to marry his sister-in-law, Herodias, wife of his half-brother Philip (not Philip the tetrarch). Herod appears to have had an interest in John and his message (Mark 6.20). After John's death, Herod began to hear about the miracles of Jesus and thought John had somehow been reincarnated.

Herod's oath was likely made in a drunken stupor and would have been absolved even by Jewish religious authorities; however, it was considered an insult to break an oath made in front of guests.

Rabbis were not expected to provide for their followers, so the disciples' desire to disperse the crowd was an effort to look out for the multitude.

The miracle of feeding the crowd showed that Jesus could provide the daily bread He had taught His disciples to pray for (6.11). He also provided abundantly as evidenced by the amount that was collected when the crowd was finished eating.

The fourth watch was between 3 and 6 a.m.

Jesus' *It is I* can also be translated *I am* and may allude to God's identification of Himself to Moses (Ex. 3.14).

INSIGHTS

Jesus responded to Peter's request to walk on water by allowing him to do so. It was only after he realized what he was doing and doubt set in that Peter began to sink. God can permit us to do what in human terms is impossible. When we find ourselves in such situations, our response should be to trust that God is at work and will continue to provide for and protect us. While God knows that we often experience doubt and uncertainty, He calls us to trust Him despite being in the midst of the impossible.

1. After Jesus fed the over 5,000 people, the disciples gather 12 baskets of leftover food—a lesson for each disciple perhaps? Have you thought that what you have to offer is far too small to meet the need? Are you willing to trust God to do more than you can imagine with the little you have when you offer it to Him? When was the last time you were amazed at what God did with the little that seemed to be available?

2. The minute Peter let fear get between him and Jesus, he began to sink. Jesus does not want us to live in fear but to live a life of faith in Him. He will not let us sink!! How does fear get in the way of your faith?

MATTHEW 15

BACKGROUND

Over time, an oral tradition based on the Law of Moses developed. This tradition defined and extended the Law by giving examples and commenting on specifics not found in the Law. As time passed, many religious leaders placed more emphasis on the oral tradition than they did on the Law itself. One tradition allowed people to dedicate possessions to God, thereby making them available for their own use, but not for anyone else. In this way, people could avoid honoring their parents in their old age as the fourth Commandment required (Deut. 5.16).

OVERVIEW

An indication of the extent to which Jesus' reputation had spread can be seen in the Pharisees' and scribes' willingness to travel from Jerusalem to Galilee in order to see Him.

Hand washing was done for ceremonial cleansing purposes rather than for hygiene. It was one of the traditions that had been incorporated over time but was not required for anyone other than priests.

Jesus quoted Isaiah (29.13) who testified to a time when the people would merely give lip service to God, rather than worship with their deeds and actions.

The cleansing requirements included in the Law of Moses were designed to draw people to repentance for their sins as they symbolically cleansed themselves outwardly. By Jesus' time, many of the religious leaders had lost sight of the Law's intent and focused instead simply on adhering to it, allowing it to become empty ritual instead of meaningful preparation for worship.

In explaining His parable, Jesus pointed to the true cause of uncleanness in a person: his or her thoughts. As a result, it was thoughts coming out of a person, not lack of ritual cleaning or things ingested that defiled a person.

A *woman of Canaan* was a Gentile. Though she had no claim as a Jew, she was likely well aware of Jesus' reputation as a healer.

Jesus' statement that He came for the lost sheep of Israel was not a definitive statement about whom He had come to minister to. Israel was God's chosen people, and Jesus gave them the first opportunity to respond. However, His message was not intended solely for the Jewish people. He had already healed several Gentiles and taught many more.

Though Jesus had gained a reputation for healing miraculously, to see so many people on the mountainside receive healing would have been an astonishing sight even for those who believed miracles occurred.

The feeding of the four thousand was a separate event from the feeding of the five thousand (14.14-21). The second miracle showed that providing for the people was not the result of supernatural happenstance. Rather, it was something Jesus could do at will. Jesus Himself referred to the two events later when speaking to the disciples (16.9-10).

INSIGHTS

God has always been more concerned with the state and attitude of our hearts than with the ritual practices in which we might engage. Jesus' response to the Pharisees (what comes out of one's mouth is of greater importance than what goes in) confirmed this. Samuel did the same when he rebuked Saul for keeping animals to sacrifice to God instead of destroying them as God had decreed (1 Sam. 15.22). We can be tempted to think that performing a ritual or repeating a rote prayer will satisfy God. In fact, what He desires is our heart—our honesty before Him and our obedience to Him. These mean far more than any ritual.

1. In Jesus' time, the Pharisees believed that only external things made you clean or unclean. Jesus tried to broaden their perspective by pointing out that what we say and do comes from the condition of our hearts, not from external factors. Have you ever examined yourself to determine the condition of your heart? Have you asked God to reveal to you the places where your heart is hard toward Him and show you how to soften those places?

2. The Canaanite woman was persistent in her faith, pursuing Jesus until He healed her daughter. How persistent are you in bringing your troubles to the Lord?

3. Jesus is compassionate towards our needs, often meeting them in abundance if we let Him work in our lives. Do you bring your needs to Jesus with the expectation that He will meet them? How have you seen Him work in your life in surprising or unimaginable ways?

Matthew 16

BACKGROUND

Caesarea Philippi was located at the more important of the two sources of the Jordan River. It was built by Herod Philip (one of Herod the Great's sons who ruled after his death) and named after Caesar with Philip's name added to differentiate it from Caesarea. It was located twenty miles north of the Sea of Galilee at the base of Mt. Hermon. The city had a long history of pagan worship that took place at an immense stone facade carved to house several different idols.

OVERVIEW

Heaven was also a Jewish title for God, so the Pharisees and Sadducees may have been requesting a sign from God. Signs in the Old Testament had sometimes been dramatic, such as the fire from heaven in response to Elijah's prayer (1 Kin. 18.36-38). More often they were much less dramatic, such as when God commanded Ezekiel to use an iron plate to represent the coming siege of Jerusalem (Ezek. 4.3).

Part of the stone facade at Caesarea Philippi. Personal photo

Leaven was sometimes used as a symbol of evil in Jewish tradition. Jesus used the symbolism to describe the doctrines of the Pharisees and Sadducees, which included legalism, political opportunism, and hypocrisy.

All the answers the disciples gave as to who Jesus was were prophets. Though common belief among the Jews was that prophets had ceased to exist, many expected a prophet to come at the end times.

Though Peter's understanding of who Jesus was had been revealed by God, he still had a lot to learn about what it meant that He was the Christ (16.22).

The disciples, along with the rest of the Jewish population, were waiting expectantly for the Messiah who would re-establish the Jewish nation. They were not looking for a Messiah who would come to bring a new church.

Matthew was the only gospel writer to use the word *church*.

Up until Jesus gave Simon the name *Peter,* which means "rock," Peter had not been used as a proper name. Some believe Jesus' statement, *on this rock I will build my church*, means Peter was to be the head of the new church. Others believe Jesus meant He was establishing His church on Peter's confession that Jesus was the Christ.

The *kingdom of heaven* is used consistently to refer to the coming future kingdom. Through ongoing divine guidance and Jesus' teaching, Peter would be given the authority (for which keys were symbolic) to determine who was admitted into the kingdom and who was not.

The statement *from that time* marks a turning point in Jesus' ministry. The earlier part of Jesus' ministry had been focused on teaching His message and training the apostles. His ministry now focused on the journey to Jerusalem and the cross.

See the Son of Man coming in His kingdom is thought to anticipate the Transfiguration, in which Jesus was seen in a glorified state. The *some standing here* would seem to verify this as only Peter, James, and John, not all the disciples, saw Jesus during the Transfiguration.

INSIGHTS

Just as God chose to reveal to Peter the true identity of Jesus, so He may periodically divinely reveal truths to us. We should not assume, however, that the revelation means we completely understand God's message. Peter was able to state what had been revealed to him, but he still needed to understand the full implications of that truth. Only time and the continued unfolding of God's plan finally made the entire truth evident. Likewise, God's revelations to us may need time and the further unfolding of His plan to be understood fully. In the meantime, we can trust God to continue what He has started in us (Phil. 1.6).

1. Jesus warned the disciples about the yeast of the Pharisees and Sadducees. This still applies to us today. We must be on guard against those who falsely teach God's word. When you question a statement or teaching you have heard, what do you use to discover the truth? How often do you use scripture to help you discern truth from lies?

2. How do you feel about denying yourself and taking up your cross in order to follow Jesus? Jesus wants us to follow Him with total commitment, even if it means death. Here death does not refer only to physical death but to the death of habits, relationships, and things that distract us from following after Jesus. Where is your level of commitment to Jesus? Are you willing to make the necessary changes in order to follow Jesus wholeheartedly?

Matthew 17

BACKGROUND

The temple tax was collected annually from all Jewish men over the age of twenty (Ex. 30.13-16) and used for the temple's upkeep. During the time of Moses, the tax was half a shekel. By the time of Jesus, the half-shekel coin was no longer being used and two drachmas were used instead. Both amounts were equivalent to approximately two days' wages. After 70 A.D., the Romans confiscated the tax and used it to pay for upkeep of a pagan temple.

OVERVIEW

Moses and Elijah were both expected to return. Their presence with Jesus during the Transfiguration was another indication that the Old Testament scriptures were being fulfilled in Jesus.

This is My beloved Son in whom I am well pleased are the same words spoken when Jesus was baptized (3.17). *Hear Him* is an allusion to Moses' statement that a prophet from among the people would be raised up. The people were to listen to him. (Deut.18.15).

An Old Testament scripture stated that Elijah would return before the day of judgment (Mal. 4.5-6). Jesus' use of *will restore* and *has come* has led many to believe the prophecy was partially fulfilled in Jesus' time and is yet to be completely fulfilled. As the three apostles discerned, John the Baptist fulfilled part of the prophecy associated with Elijah (Mal.3.1). Some have speculated that one of the two witnesses in the apostle John's vision (Rev. 11.3-6) will bring about the future fulfillment of this prophecy.

In Jesus' absence, the remaining disciples had attempted to do what Jesus had given them the power to do. Their inability to do so came from their lack of faith in God's ability to work through them. Mountains were viewed as one of the most stable objects in the world, while a mustard seed was analogous to a very small amount. Thus God would give the ability to do whatever He asked, provided the disciples trusted God.

Not only are prayer and fasting ways of discerning God's will, but they are also a means of beseeching God to defeat the enemy. They are a reminder that victory over the enemy does not come cheaply.

Jesus attempted to prepare His disciples for His coming death and resurrection by repeatedly warning them of the impending events. The disciples did not grasp the significance of the resurrection as is evident by their great sorrow following the announcement.

As the Son of God, Jesus implied He was free from paying the temple tax. His plural use of *sons* indicates that Peter and the other disciples were also excused from paying it.

INSIGHTS

The disciples were unable to cast out the demon because of their lack of faith. God can overcome any opposition from Satan and makes this same power available to us, though we must first have faith in Him. Some have distorted this relationship between God's power and our faith in Him by implying that any bad that comes our way (illness, lack of prosperity, loss of a job, etc.) happens because we do not have enough faith. God's will always takes precedent. Even when we have great faith and pray for something that would seem to be godly (such as healing for a sick child), God may choose not to in order to bring about His plan.

1. Jesus allowed three of his disciples to witness His transfiguration as a means of encouraging their belief and faith. How do you make yourself available to see God's glory so you can be encouraged?

2. Jesus told his disciples they only need faith the size of a small mustard seed to see and do great things for God's kingdom. Why do you think such small faith can do such big things? How big is your faith?

3. Jesus specializes in doing the impossible to awe and encourage us. Put yourself in the scene where Jesus told Peter to find the money for the temple tax in a fish's mouth. Imagine what Peter must have thought and felt. How do you respond when God directs you to do the seemingly impossible?

Matthew 18

BACKGROUND

Matthew contains five discourses (Matt. 5-7, 10, 13, 18, 23-25) spoken by Jesus. Chapter 18 contains the fourth of these. The focus is on humility, which Jesus taught was necessary for five reasons.

- It is needed to gain entrance into heaven (vs. 2-3).
- It is a measure of greatness in the coming kingdom (v. 4).
- It is a reliable tool for preventing stumbling, sin, and tempting others (vs. 5-11).
- It allows individuals to carry out the work of the church (vs. 12-20).
- It is essential to forgiving as God forgives. (vs. 21-35).

OVERVIEW

Rank and social status were important issues in ancient Jewish and Roman cultures. Jesus implied there would be some sort of rank in heaven (5.19).

Children had the lowest rank in the Jewish culture. They were loved and any power or status came through that love. Thus Jesus implied that any power or status believers had in the coming kingdom would come through the love of the Father rather than through any personal standing one had. Jesus was not suggesting that people be childish in their faith but childlike. The qualities found in children, trust, honesty, openness, lack of self-sufficiency, should also be found in people of faith.

The Greek word for millstone refers to the heaviest kind moved by a donkey rather than the lighter millstone used by women. This type of punishment would have been attributed to pagans and would have been quite shocking.

Cutting off a hand/foot or plucking out an eye was not meant literally, but referred to the drastic measures and painful sacrifices that were sometimes required for those who live in sin.

An average flock was about one hundred animals. The flock would have been left in the care of assistant shepherds while the head shepherd went in search of the missing sheep. The image is analogous to God's efforts to ensure that all people who are lost come under His protection.

Jesus outlined a process for addressing a believer who had fallen into sin. Each step gave the fallen believer an opportunity to respond. The goal of the process was/is to draw the believer away from his/her sinful choices and back into fellowship with the church and God. Should the fallen believer fail to respond, s/he was to be treated like an unbeliever (heathen). In Jewish culture, heathens (those who did not believe in the Jewish faith) and tax collectors (viewed as agents of the pagan government) were excluded from Jewish religious life. Such loss of fellowship would have been painful for the offender.

Jesus stated that *whatever,* not whoever, would be bound or loosened. This refers to actions that are judged as permitted or not permitted.

Taken in context, *two or three gathered* refers to the issue of seeking guidance for discipline. God is present even to one person who prays. He promises to provide guidance when two or more gather to confront and seek restoration with a sinning brother/sister.

A denarius was equivalent to a day's wage and six thousand equaled one talent. Therefore, ten thousand talents was an exorbitant amount—sixty million days' wages and more than any person could repay.

The point of the parable is that believers have been forgiven all of their sins; an enormous debt they can never repay. As a result, each should be willing to extend forgiveness for the smaller debt incurred due to the sin of those around them.

INSIGHTS

Extending forgiveness to the murder of a family member, a trusted business partner who ruins our reputation, or a con artist who swindles an elderly parent out of their life savings can be incredibly hard. Some offenses seem too big to forgive. To God, we have all committed similar and countless offenses against Him. Sin is only black and white to God, no little white lies or gray areas. Yet God extends forgiveness to each of us as we place our trust and faith in Christ. Even though it can be too difficult to imagine, God asks us to extend the same forgiveness and will give us the strength and courage to do what He calls us to.

1. Jesus tells us that to become great in the kingdom of heaven, we must be like little children who are humble and trusting. Is your belief like that of a child? How can you develop childlike faith?

2. In the parable of the lost sheep we see how joy-filled God is over our salvation. Though willing to pursue us in our wandering, God's desire is for us to be found. Should we be as concerned for lost souls as God is? Where is your heart for the lost around you? Do you desire to show Jesus to them so they might be saved?

3. Jesus tells us to forgive our brothers again and again. Are you holding unforgiveness toward someone in your heart?

Matthew 19

BACKGROUND

An *inclusio* is a literary device used to bracket or mark a portion of text. This device is used throughout the Old and New Testaments, though it is sometimes harder to recognize in English translations. An *inclusio* can take several forms. It might be a repeated phrase at the beginning and end of a parable, a question posed at the beginning and end of a series of events or a statement that is stated one way at the beginning and in reverse order at the end. See Ps. 8.1,9 for an example.

OVERVIEW

The question of who could divorce and for what reasons centered around the definition of uncleanness (Deut. 24.1). The topic had long been debated and several schools of thought existed in Jesus' time. The Pharisees, however, approached Jesus with malicious intent, as evidenced by the use of the word *testing*. Jesus replied by referring to God's original intent for marriage (Gen. 1.27; 2.24): God created one man and one woman, marriage is the strongest bond of all human relationships, and the physical union of a man and woman is representative of their union in all areas of their lives. To divorce meant not only impairing the very core of human unity—it separated or took apart what God had joined together.

The Pharisees challenged Jesus' conclusions by referring to Moses' approval to write a certificate of divorce for a wife who was found with uncleanness. Such approval was given because of humanity's hard-heartedness, not because it met God's ideals in any way. Jesus emphasized God's ideal and warned His listeners of the consequences that resulted from not striving to live up to that ideal.

It is interesting to note the sequence of the topics in this and the previous chapter. The question of divorce was raised after Jesus gave His discourse on forgiveness.

Celibacy can be the result of a birth defect, imposition by others, or a choice one makes for himself. These cases, however, are not the norm, but should be accepted when appropriate.

Jesus' response to the rich young man included the human directed mandates of the Ten Commandments (as opposed to the God directed mandates). Further, Jesus' response was not an endorsement of salvation through works. Instead, He was challenging the rich young man's claim to have fulfilled God's law. If he truly loved his neighbors as himself, he would have had no difficulty in selling his possession in order to help those in need.

Just as it would be impossible for a camel to literally go through the eye of a needle, so it was impossible for the rich (or any human for that matter) to enter the kingdom of heaven through their own efforts. This did not mean the situation was hopeless. What is impossible for humanity is well within the scope of the possible for God.

Regeneration was a Greek term used to refer to the future renewal of the world. Since Jews believed the world would be renewed when the promised kingdom came, the term fit into their expectations as well.

Jesus promised the disciples that their efforts to serve Him and those to whom He would send them would not be made in vain. They would receive their reward in heaven.

The last verse of this chapter rightfully belongs with the parable that begins the next chapter. It serves as an *inclusion* or bracket, along with 20.16, marking the beginning and end of the parable.

INSIGHTS

Peter's question about what he and the other disciples could expect because they had given up all to follow Jesus may seem selfish at first glance. Throughout the gospels, Jesus continually stated there would be a reward for being obedient to God. In fact, the entire Bible reiterates this fact. Given that God has promised such a reward, it is not selfish for each of us to live our lives in a manner that will maximize that reward. To do so means to live humble lives before God, seek His will in all we do, have hearts after His own and be obedient to all He calls us to. This is just the kind of life God would desire us to live (Micah 6:8).

1. Jesus told his listeners it is hard for a rich man to enter God's kingdom. This is because we find it so difficult to give up earthly possessions in exchange for heavenly treasures. Are you able to let go of your earthly possessions to follow Jesus more closely? If you struggle in this area, do not lose hope. Jesus reminds us that *with God all things are possible.* He will help you if you ask!

2. God created the bonds of marriage to last for a lifetime. Yet just as divorce was a part of the culture in Jesus' time, so it is part of our culture. Divorce can be a difficult topic within the church, which often stigmatizes those who have divorced. If you have been affected by divorce, how have you asked God to be in the midst of your circumstances? He can comfort and heal you and redeem your experience.

Matthew 20

BACKGROUND

In Jesus' time, the day began at sunrise, which occurred about 6 a.m. Because the days often got quite hot, work would begin early in the morning while temperatures were still cool. Time was counted by the hours that had passed since sunrise. The following times are approximate.

- Third hour - 9 a.m.
- Sixth hour - Noon
- Ninth hour - 3 p.m.
- Eleventh hour - 5 p.m.

OVERVIEW

The landowner agreed to the standard wage, one denarius, for the initial workers he hired. No such agreement was made with the remaining workers hired later in the day. These workers trusted the landowner to be fair.

When the landowner paid those who had worked only one hour a full day's wage, the initial workers thought they would be rewarded with more than a day's wage. Their grumbling response at receiving no more than what had been agreed upon was due to their envious nature (evil eye). The landowner suggested they should appreciate his generous nature instead.

The statement about first and last that opened this parable was repeated in reverse order at the parable's end.

The initial workers represented the Jewish nation, who had the covenants (contracts) with God. The later workers represented the Gentiles, who would receive the same salvation as the Jewish people when they placed their faith in Christ.

Jesus again referred to His death and resurrection. For the first time, He indicated the manner in which He would die.

Though James and John respond in the affirmative when asked if they could share in the cup and baptism of Jesus, they likely did not fully understand what they were being asked. The *cup* represented Jesus' coming death.

The displeasure of the remaining disciples was likely motivated by their own hidden desire to occupy the same spots James and John's mother had requested for her sons.

Jesus' disciples wanted to measure greatness in humanity's standard terms: position, power, and prestige. Jesus made it clear that true greatness came from service to others.

Mark (10.46-52) and Luke (18.35-43) both mention only one blind man on the road to Jericho, while Matthew mentions two. It is possible that Mark and Luke mention only the man who spoke. It is appropriate that Matthew writes about two blind men. Matthew's Gospel was written to a Jewish audience, who would have preferred two witnesses to verify the incident (Deut. 19.15).

The men's use of *Son of David*, meaning Messiah, shows their spiritual insight, even as they lacked physical sight.

INSIGHTS

Jesus' parable illustrates that the desire for things to be fair is a part of human nature. It is important to look beyond the fairness of an issue to what God is doing. God is much less concerned about things being fair than He is about people entering eternal life. This is evident in His own Son's life. It was not fair that Jesus, the only sinless human to ever live, was falsely accused, condemned, and suffered one of the most torturous deaths known to humanity. The result of this "unfairness," however, was eternal life for all who believe in Jesus. In a similar manner, God may well use "unfairness" in our own lives to bring redemption to others.

1. The parable of the workers is an amazing story of God's mercy. All who believe will share in the same reward, even the latecomers! How do you feel about this truth? Are you angry like the early workers? Or excited to see others join you in God's great kingdom? Is there any jealousy you need to repent of and ask God's forgiveness for?

2. Jesus gave clear instructions on how to become great in His kingdom by serving others. Jesus set the greatest example by sacrificing His life on our behalf so that we may experience eternal life with Him, even though we are completely undeserving. He calls us to follow His example, though rarely to the point of death. Where is your heart for serving? Are you more self-focused or others-focused?

Matthew 21

BACKGROUND

The Kidron valley is directly between the Mt. of Olives and the eastern wall of Jerusalem. From the Mt. of Olives, where Jesus often went to pray, He could see over the city wall and view the Temple. Jesus later agonized over His coming crucifixion in the Garden of Gethsemane in the Kidron Valley. *Gethsemane*, meaning *oil press,* refers to a location where olives were processed. Some believe this was an appropriate place for Jesus to go the night before He was *pressed* through crucifixion.

OVERVIEW

Bethphage was located on the eastern slope of the Mt. of Olives and across the Kidron Valley from Jerusalem.

Jesus' entry into Jerusalem was the fulfillment of the prophecy found in Zechariah 9.9.

Donkeys were used for civil, not military, processions. By using a donkey, Jesus was not entering the city in military triumph, but as a peaceful and humble king.

Previous to Jesus' grand procession into Jerusalem, He avoided such displays and withdrew when faced with opposition.

Pilgrims making their way to the temple often could not easily transport the required animals for their sacrifices. As a result, animals were available for purchase at the temple. Moneychangers were also needed because many cities had their own currencies, so pilgrims needed the ability to exchange their money for local currency. Jesus was not protesting the need for either of these groups and their services.

Rather, He was decrying the corruption that had come to accompany the transactions. Jesus quoted from Isaiah 56.7 and Jeremiah 7.11 as He made His accusation.

The chief priests and scribes could not deny that healing those with physical ailments was wonderful, but the perceived threat to their positions and the temple culture outweighed the good they witnessed.

The withered fig tree was Jesus' only miracle involving judgment. Some have taken it as an illustration of Jerusalem and its temple, which looked nice but did not produce spiritual fruit.

It was common in Jewish debates to answer one question with another. The chief priests and elders' refusal to answer Jesus' question released Him from answering theirs and exposed the hollowness of their spiritual leadership.

Jesus' question regarding the two sons illustrates God's pleasure with those who obey Him, even if it takes a while to repent and follow Him. Tax collectors and harlots were considered among the most unprincipled and immoral. That they would enter the kingdom of heaven first does not exclude the religious leaders from also entering. They simply needed to repent.

The parable of the wicked vinedressers represents the nation of Israel and their response to God. God, as the landowner, provided for His vineyard. The vinedressers represented the nation of Israel, who were supposed to produce fruit by being a witness to surrounding nations. The servants were God's prophets, who were not treated well and were often killed by the nation. The son is Jesus, the long anticipated Messiah.

The rejection of the son was predicted in Ps. 118.22-23, which Jesus quoted.

Nation refers to the church, which today bears the fruit (though not perfectly) that Israel was supposed to bear. Because of God's promises to Abraham, David, and others, Israel is not entirely removed from God's plans and will one day be restored.

INSIGHTS

Just as the chief priests and scribes were so set in their ways they were unwilling to be swayed by the evidence before them, so we can miss God's work in our midst. God is always at work around us, sometimes for our benefit, other times for the benefit of those around us. We can choose to be closed to the evidence around us and miss God at work. On the other hand, we can be open-minded to the evidence of God's work and allow it to help us discern His will for our lives. This can further allow us to join in God's work and advance His kingdom to the ends of the earth.

1. In this chapter, Jesus fulfilled Zechariah's prophecy by riding into Jerusalem on a donkey (Zech. 9.9). What are some of the other prophecies Jesus has fulfilled? What are some of the prophecies we are waiting for Him to fulfill? Did you know that Dr. Peter Stoner[2] calculated the odds of one man fulfilling just eight of the more than 300 prophecies about a messiah at 1 in 10^{17}?

2. Jesus used the parable of the sons asked to work in the vineyard as a means of communicating who would be eligible for His plan of salvation. Many Jews of the time thought that only they were God's chosen people and thus would receive the promised eternal life. The thought that Gentiles would receive the same gift simply by believing Jesus was completely foreign to the Jews. This means that even our worst enemy may one day join us in heaven if they accept Jesus as their Savior. Is this God's justice or mercy?

[2] Peter Stoner, *Science Speaks* (Chicago: Moody Press, 1958)

MATTHEW 22

BACKGROUND

In Biblical times weddings involved numerous steps. First, a marriage contract was made and the couple became engaged. About a year later, the actual wedding took place. The groom was presented with the bride at the bride's house. This was followed by a nighttime procession to the groom's house, where the wedding feast was held. The feast could last for a week and all the guests were expected to stay until it was concluded.

OVERVIEW

It was common practice to tell parables in which God was compared to a king. In this parable, the son represents Jesus. The wedding feast represents the coming kingdom of God. The invited guests represent the nation of Israel, who spurned God's covenant with them and killed or persecuted many of His prophets. The good and bad people likely refer to both Jews and Gentiles, some of whom were morally good and others morally evil. The wedding garments represent the preparation believers can do on earth before entering into the coming kingdom (i.e. obedience to God, doing the work of advancing His kingdom, etc.).

A preliminary invitation (similar to modern day "save the date" announcements) was customarily sent so guests would have no excuse for not attending. A second invitation was sent out telling the guests the banquet was ready and they should come right away.

The Herodians (supporters of Herod's dynasty in collaboration with the Roman government) and Pharisees (Jewish nationalists) were at opposite ends of the political spectrum. Both were threatened by Jesus and united in an effort to rid themselves of Him. As Jesus answered the question, he risked being accused of insurrection (for not paying tax to the Roman government) or losing favor with the masses (for supporting a tax that was paid to the oppressor). Instead of suggesting the people *pay* the tax, Jesus said they should *render*, meaning "pay back" (give back) the tax, thereby supporting the obligation the people had to both the ruling government and the kingdom of God.

It was common to propose hypothetical situations in an attempt to further define Jewish law. In response to the Sadducees, Jesus pointed out that God could not be the God of the patriarchs if they were dead.

Jesus changed the *heart, soul, and might/strength* of Deuteronomy 6.5 to *heart, soul and mind*. In either case, the three represented the whole person. The commandment placed God as the priority in the believer's life. People naturally love themselves and, therefore, seek the best for themselves. The second commandment directed people to apply the same standards to looking out for the welfare of others as for oneself.

In essence, Jesus' question to the Pharisees was a puzzle: how could the coming Messiah be both David's descendant and David's God? Jesus quoted from a psalm written by David (110.1), which, according to Jesus, was written under the inspiration of the Holy Spirit.

INSIGHTS

As the wedding feast parable implies, God desires us to do more than just put our faith in Christ. Doing so will certainly gain us eternal life (and like the thief on the cross, may be all some are able to do). Yet God forbids us to live lives of self-indulgent pleasure and neglect those who have yet to hear the message of hope. Just as Jesus' conversation with the rich young man made clear, great reward awaits all those who are willing to make God a priority in their lives. Doing so may involve hardship, suffering, and sacrifice, but none of it will go unnoticed by the God who pays attention to every detail.

1. God wants all of us at His banquet, but unfortunately, not all choose to say yes to His invitation. Have you accepted God's invitation? How has God pursued you or how is He pursuing you in the hopes that you, too, will be seated at his banquet table?

2. Both of God's greatest commandments involve love. How have you loved God lately? How well do you love your neighbor?

MATTHEW 23

BACKGROUND

Phylacteries are small boxes containing scripture that are bound to one's head and left hand with a leather strap. The scripture verses in the boxes were recited as part of the morning and evening prayers. The practice is based on several passages in the Old Testament, including Exodus 13.16 and Deuteronomy 6.8.

OVERVIEW

The Pharisees and scribes taught the scriptures as they were written. However, they tended to be very legalistic and put greater priority on their own rules and regulations. Jesus warned His hearers to be cautious. They should follow the teachings of the Pharisees and scribes but not their example (i.e. actions). Their meticulous appearance covered hearts full of envy, pride, and self-importance.

Borders (some translations) referred to the tassels Israelites wore on the hem of their garments to remind them of God's laws (Num. 15.37-41). In order to appear especially holy and righteous, some Pharisees would make their phylacteries quite large and their tassels quite long.

The prohibition against using the titles *rabbi*, *father*, and *teacher* was not universal. The titles are used elsewhere in scripture with no qualification. Jesus was condemning the use of the titles as a show of prestige and power.

Woes is a form of prayer found in the Old Testament. The woes Jesus pronounced on the Pharisees and scribes were motivated by their blatant opposition to the truth. Such opposition was not only directed toward Jesus but toward much of the scribes and Pharisees' interpretation of the scriptures as well. Jesus spoke of the oaths the scribes and Pharisees stated were not binding (sworn by the temple, altar, and heaven) vs. the oaths they said were binding (sworn by the gold of the temple, the gift on the altar, and God). God, on the other hand, had stated in the Old Testament that all oaths were binding and they should only be made if one intended to keep them (Num. 30.2; Zech. 8.17). Seven of the eight woes named the scribes and Pharisees specifically while one woe referred to them as blind guides.

Sons of hell is thought to be a Hebrew expression referring to a wicked person. It would likely be opposite of *sons of the kingdom* (13.38).

Jesus accused the scribes and Pharisees of being meticulous about tithing on the smallest of items such as mint, dill (anise), and cumin, but neglecting other weightier (more burdensome) parts of the law such as justice, mercy, and faith. His accusation did not mean tithing was unimportant, but that more weight was put on one part of the law than another, when all parts were equally important.

A person's character was represented by the inside of a cup. The scribes and Pharisees went to great lengths to ensure they looked good to all who would see them but paid little or no attention to what was happening in their hearts. The image of the whitewashed tombs portrayed a similar concept.

The Hebrew Scriptures are ordered differently to those found in the Christian Old Testament. In the Hebrew order of the scriptures, Abel was the first person to be murdered (as in the Christian Old Testament; Gen. 4.8), while Zechariah was the last (2 Chr. 24.20-22).

INSIGHTS

God did not give us the scriptures to be a burden as the scribes and Pharisees' interpretation and legalistic approach often created. Instead, God gave us the scriptures for our protection, to maximize our enjoyment of life and to allow us to experience fulfillment in life. This does not mean that being obedient will not at times be burdensome (choosing what is right instead of following the crowd), unenjoyable (dealing with illness in oneself, family member, or friend), or unfulfilling (parenting a wayward child). Yet God honors our obedience and rewards us both in this life and the next, even when life is less than what we hoped for.

1. Jesus was clear about how He felt regarding the hypocrisy in the hearts of those who were teachers of the law. We must be cautious about falling into the same trap. Are there any areas where you might be performing for men instead of serving God alone?

2. Jesus wants us to be honest about ourselves inside and out. He also wants us to represent Him well. Are you a person of integrity? Or do you make yourself look good on the outside as you struggle with a sinful heart? If you are struggling, ask God to help you be the man/woman He wants you to be.

Matthew 24

BACKGROUND

The temple was central to Jewish life. The community, as well as some commerce, revolved around the religious activities that took place in the temple. Its massive size, beautiful appearance, and solid construction gave the impression it was indestructible. For many Jews, the destruction of the temple was unthinkable, even though Jeremiah and other prophets had foretold such an eventuality (Jer. 7.4-15). The temple was completed in 64 A.D. and destroyed only six years later by the Romans.

Jesus elaborated on the end times in the apostle John's vision recorded in Revelation.

OVERVIEW

Though some of the giant stones still remain from the temple, the destruction Jesus foretold (using hyperbole for emphasis) was so complete that today, the exact location of the sanctuary is unknown.

The disciples thought the destruction of the temple and the end times would occur at the same time.

Because the world will one day be ruled by one sinful man (the antichrist), believers throughout the world will experience persecution. Many will not withstand the persecution. They will renounce their faith in Christ and follow the ways of pagan religions. Yet despite the lawlessness that will prevail and stifle love, God's word will continue to be spoken.

Although some believed Jesus' prophecy was coming to pass with the destruction of the temple in 70 A.D. and fled to the mountains surrounding Judea, the prophecy has yet to be filled.

Jesus warned His listeners not to be fooled by false messiahs who would perform great signs for purposes of deceiving unbelievers and even believers. Such signs have to be judged against correct doctrine. Other signs would be promised but fail to materialize.

Unlike Jesus' first coming, which occurred very quietly, His second coming will be hard to miss.

Some believe the *sign of the Son of Man* will be a heavenly appearance of a cross while others believe it will be Jesus Himself.

The trumpet will be used to gather God's elect. This gathering is likely the nation of Israel, which is repeatedly prophesied in the Old Testament (Is. 11.11-12; Jer. 16.14-15; Ezek. 34.13).

Speculation has revolved around what *this generation* refers to. Some believe it means *race*; in other words, while some ancient civilizations no longer exist (Hittites), the Jewish people will continue to exist until all Jesus has stated has come to pass. Other believe it means that the last elements of the end times will occur so quickly, one generation will see the antichrist, the tribulation, and the return of Christ.

As God, Jesus would know the day and the hour when He would return. As incarnate man, He surrendered some of His divine attributes (knowledge of the future) and took on some human attributes (hunger and thirst).

Eating, drinking, and marrying are not sinful activities. Just as the people of Noah's time engaged in such activities, yet were indifferent to God and were judged, so indifference to Christ will be judged. Vigilance, not indifference, is needed to avoid judgment.

Absentee owners often put servants in charge of their households. Those servants who manage their masters' affairs well in his absence will be rewarded while those who abuse their position will suffer judgment.

INSIGHTS

Since Jesus' time, many people have claimed to be the messiah or a prophet of God. Some have been able to perform miracles, such as healing, while others have claimed to have knowledge belonging only to God (such as the date and time of Jesus' return). Yet, despite such abilities or claims, the motivation of these people can be far from godly. The only sure way to avoid being deceived is to have intimate knowledge of God's Word and continually seek the leading of the Holy Spirit. Measuring a modern-day prophet's words and actions against God's Word and the Holy Spirit will give us great discernment.

1. We hear many stories in our day and age about the time when Christ will return. In this chapter, Jesus warns us not to be deceived by people who think they have the answer and reminds us that only the Father knows the day He will return. Have you fallen prey to false predictions? How can you guard against doing so?

2. Jesus warns us to be ready for His return. How have you prepared for His return? Are you ready if today is the day? If not, consider doing those things God lays on your heart to get ready.

Matthew 25

BACKGROUND

The Book of Matthew has sometimes been referred to as the "Gospel of Judgment" because the writer communicated so much about the topic. Matthew's gospel looks to the coming kingdom and what is required for admittance. As a result, it is not surprising that the topic of judgment appears so frequently (3.12; 6.2, 5, 16; 7.24-27; 13.30, 47-49; 18.23-34; 20.1-16; 21.33-41; 22.1-14; 24.45-51; 25.1-12, 14-46).

OVERVIEW

Jesus moved through a series of parables, which began with the good servant who was faithful and wise (24.45-51). This was followed by the need for vigilance and wisdom (25.1-13) and the need for faithfulness (25.14-29).

The ten virgins were waiting for the procession from the bride's house to the groom's. Sharing oil would have left very little for anyone and potentially ruined the wedding procession.

Just as a wedding was announced well in advance of the event, so Christ's return has also been announced. Adequate time has been given to make the necessary preparations. Those who choose not to prepare will forfeit the opportunity to participate.

The master gave to each of his servants according to their ability and expected them to perform according to that ability. They were each given a small fortune. One talent represented approximately sixteen years labor for the average worker.

The master judged his servants on their faithfulness. As a result, the first two received the same reward even though they were given different amounts to work with. The last servant had ability but allowed fear to paralyze him from taking any meaningful action. He mistook his master's intentions and chose to act safely instead of performing the service his master expected.

One of God's standards of judgment centers on one's willingness to meet the needs of others. Needs constantly present themselves so lack of opportunity can never be an excuse.

Every person was created by God and carries the image of God within themselves. Therefore, tending to the needs of any person is, in effect, caring for God Himself.

The same Greek word, translated *eternal,* is used to describe the judgment given to both the unrighteous and the righteous. Repeated use of this term indicates that one will last as long as the other.

INSIGHTS

If we are given an object for safekeeping, being able to return it without having it stolen, wasted, or lost is judged as a good thing. By this standard, some would judge the third servant in a good light—he was able to return what had been given to him. But the master did not give the talent to the servant simply for safekeeping. The master expected his servants to use what was given to them to produce a profit. In a similar way, God gives us resources and abilities, not for safekeeping, but to produce results for His kingdom. There is a difference between the free gift of salvation by faith and eternal rewards earned through work subsequent to salvation. We will be rewarded eternally by our faithfulness in using the resources and abilities God has given us (Rev 22:12). These works are evidence of our salvation. They do not earn it.

1. The parable of the talents contrasts those who use what they have for their master's benefit with those who respond in fear. Who do you gravitate toward? Are you burying your faith and/or the spiritual gifts God has given you or are you working to use your gifts as God is directing?

2. Jesus suggests some practical ways we can help others. How are you on the lookout for how you can help those in need around you?

Matthew 26

BACKGROUND

Blood (sometimes in the form of sacrificed animals) was often used to seal a covenant (Gen. 15. 9-18; Ex. 24.8). The promise of a new covenant between God and His people is repeatedly stated in the Old Testament (Jer. 31.31-34; 32.37-40; Ezek. 37.26). Jesus' statement, "This is my blood of the new covenant" was the fulfillment of that promise.

OVERVIEW

Testing Jesus through logic and argument had not produced the desired results, so the chief priests, scribes, and elders (the Sanhedrin) had to resort to trickery.

The perfume used to anoint Jesus was likely worth a year's wages. It may have been kept as a family heirloom until it was used to anoint Jesus. The disciples looked only at the immediate context (the cost of the perfume) because they did not as yet understand the greater significance of what was occurring (anointing for burial).

Judas betrayed his master for an inexpensive price. Thirty pieces of silver was the average cost of a slave.

Jesus had been preparing His disciples for His coming death by repeatedly mentioning it. This was the first time He indicated He would be betrayed.

Though God's plan was fulfilled through Jesus' death, Judas was still responsible for betraying the Son of Man.

Three times, Jesus singled out Peter, James, and John to accompany

Him (17.1-13; 26.37; Lk. 8.49-56).

In the Old Testament, *cup* was often used to mean wrath (Is. 51.17).

Though Peter had promised not to forsake Jesus, his desertion began when he was unable to stay awake and support Jesus in prayer.

Jesus wanted the disciples not only to pray for Him but for themselves as well. Jesus knew they, too, would be severely tested in the coming hours.

Jesus knew the depths of agony He would experience as He went through the crucifixion, yet He was determined to do the will of His Father.

Despite knowing what lay ahead, Jesus still called Judas, his betrayer, "friend."

A legion was six thousand men; twelve legions would have been 72,000 angels—an unstoppable force.

Though Peter lacked courage to stay with Jesus during His arrest, he did show some courage as he followed Jesus as far as the high priest's courtyard. Such a residence would normally have been guarded and likely had increased guards given the circumstances.

In an attempt to get at the truth, the high priest put Jesus *under oath of the living God.* It is ironic that the high priest was unwittingly invoking the very God who had sent Jesus.

Jesus' association with God may have been considered offensive, but His statement was not blasphemous.

Peter's curses were not vulgar words but curses against himself should what he said prove to be anything but the truth. Peter's bitter tears were a sign of his deep regret and genuine repentance.

INSIGHTS

Matthew's back-to-back placement of the woman with the perfume and Judas portrays a significant contrast. The unnamed woman, who likely had little contact with Jesus, treated Him as royalty, while Judas, a member of Jesus' inner circle, betrayed Him for the cost of a slave. It can be easy for us to fall into the same trap. As we grow in our faith and have years behind us in our walk with Christ, we can be tempted to take Jesus for granted. Instead of treating Him with reverence, we treat Him as if He has no great value. Jesus has given us the ultimate gift—eternal life. In all we do, we should honor Him as the royalty He is.

1. During His last meal with His disciples, Jesus provided instructions for the sacrament of Communion, which we still practice today. How do you use communion as a reminder of Jesus' sacrifice on your behalf? When was the last time you contemplated the true significance of Jesus' dying in your place so that you might be welcomed into God's family?

2. In the garden of Gethsemane, Jesus was distraught over the agony of His impending death. Although He wanted there to be another way, in the end, He submitted His will to God's plan for Him. When you are troubled, do you pour out your heart in prayer as Jesus did? Do you readily submit your will to God's plan?

Matthew 27

BACKGROUND

Jewish festivals, including Passover, were opportunities for revolutionaries and others who were disgruntled with religious leadership or Roman rule to stir up trouble. As a result, not only was Roman security increased during festivals, but the Roman governor would travel to Jerusalem (from Caesarea) in order to forestall any disturbances that might occur.

It was common practice for Roman soldiers to take the clothing of those being crucified.

OVERVIEW

The Jewish leadership was seeking the death penalty for Jesus, which they were unauthorized to carry out. Therefore, they had to make a case to the Roman governor (Pontius Pilate) that Jesus had committed a crime deserving of death.

The religious officials who had had no difficulty in convicting an innocent man were suddenly concerned with the proper way to use *blood money*. Buying a field in which to bury strangers would have been viewed as a pious act.

The quote Matthew attributed to Jeremiah is actually found in Zechariah (11.12-13). Potential explanations for this include: the words were spoken by Jeremiah but recorded by Zechariah; Jeremiah headed the prophetic books in the time of Christ and the quotation was identified by the section in which it was found rather than the specific book, and Matthew combined passages from Zechariah and Jeremiah

(19.1, 11) and attributed them to the more well known prophet.

Matthew is the only writer to record both the cautions of Pilate's wife and the governor's attempt to release himself from responsibility for the blood of an innocent man by washing his hands.

A scourging (flogging) was performed with a whip in which pieces of metal or bone were tied into the thongs. The prisoner, at a minimum, would suffer a bloodied back with strips of flesh hanging from the wounds. At worst, bone and even internal organs would be exposed. Some did not survive their scourging. For those who did, their weakened condition generally meant they could not survive as long hanging on the cross as they might have otherwise.

Gall was mixed with sour wine to form a pain-dulling liquid given to prisoners to ease their suffering. Jesus refused to drink any of it.

The prophecy fulfilled by the casting of lots for Jesus' clothing is found in Psalm 22.18.

Jesus was doing exactly what those taunting Him were suggesting. He *was* trusting in God. By staying on the cross, He was fulfilling God's plan and in the process, continuing to save others. God *would* deliver Jesus in a way no one could have expected.

The veil was the curtain that separated the Holy Place from the Holy of Holies. Humans could have ripped the veil from bottom to top, but only God could rip it from the top down. Its destruction is significant as it represented the access to God made available through the sacrifice of His Son.

Executed criminals were generally thrown into a common grave after their death. Joseph of Arimathea (a town twenty miles northwest of Jerusalem) was a prominent man to be able to get an audience with Pilate and obtain approval to bury Jesus' body.

INSIGHTS

The bystanders taunted Jesus by questioning His ability to save Himself since He said He could rebuild the destroyed temple in three days. What the bystanders failed to realize was that Jesus was in the process of doing precisely that. In the then current covenant, the temple represented God's dwelling among the people and provided them the opportunity to restore their relationship with God after sin occurred. Jesus' death and resurrection, achieved over a three-day period, created a new covenant in which God, through the Holy Spirit, would dwell within each believer and provided the means for permanent relational restoration with God.

1. The tearing of the temple curtain at the time of Jesus' death was an indication that the gift of direct access to God had been given to all who believe in Jesus. Do you know that there is nothing and no one who stands between you and God? How do you most enjoy spending time with God?

2. Jesus suffered grave injustice throughout His trial and the time leading up to His crucifixion. Jesus stated repeatedly that His suffering was an indication of the suffering His followers would also experience. Does it surprise you when suffering comes your way? How do you use your suffering as a testimony to God's goodness through your trials?

Matthew 28

BACKGROUND

In the Old Testament covenant, God called His people to be witnesses to the nations. When Jesus commissioned His disciples, He gave them a similar command; they were to go to all the nations and share the good news.

OVERVIEW

It is significant and typical of Jesus' ministry to choose women as the first witnesses of His resurrection. Women were not considered reliable witnesses, would not have been expected to be witnesses, and would not have been chosen as witnesses by anyone trying to fake Jesus' resurrection.

Two earthquakes occurred; one marked Jesus' death, while the other announced His resurrection.

After His resurrection, Jesus referred to the disciples as His brothers.

Roman guards could be executed for failing to carry out their orders. As a result, the bribe and offer of protection were fairly easy to accept.

It is interesting to note that the religious officials tried to explain the empty tomb but never attempted to deny it was empty.

It is likely that many people accompanied the disciples to Galilee. Some of the people may not have believed what had been reported had actually happened and would explain the *some doubted*.

Jesus' command was two-fold: baptize and teach. Those who were baptized were initiated into the faith while those who were taught were called to mature in their faith.

INSIGHTS

The angel told the women first to *come see* the empty tomb, then to *go tell* the disciples what they had seen. Today, God invites us to *come see*. First, we experience the good news of the gospel message. As we continue our walk with Christ, we are invited to *come see* how God can be trusted, how He works in unexpected ways, how our faith in Him is not misplaced. Each of these invitations is followed by a call to *go tell*. There is never a lack of people to tell – those who have not heard the good news; those who are discouraged; those who need their faith strengthened. In this way we can further share in the joy of the resurrection.

1. The resurrection of Jesus proves the authority and power of God. Without it there would be no Christian church. Nothing can stop God's purposes and plans. Do you believe God's plans will not fail? How do you see God's authority and power in the world around you?

2. The final verses of this chapter are called the Great Commission. They are Jesus' final charge to those of us who believe. Here is our purpose as God's chosen people: to share the good news of Jesus, to teach others about Him, and to believe He is always with us! Do you struggle to fulfill your purpose? If so, in what ways? How do you share Jesus with other people? Are you confident that Jesus is with you always? If you are not, what stands in the way of believing this truth?

MARK

John Mark is the traditionally accepted author of the Gospel of Mark. Though there is nothing in the book itself that names Mark as the author, his name circulated with the writings from the earliest times. Since the title was in use and undisputed from such an early period, there is little reason to believe Mark was not the author.

Though Mark is not recorded as one of Jesus' followers and likely was an eyewitness to only some of the events of Jesus' life, death, and resurrection, his account appears to rely heavily on the testimony of someone who actually saw the events. Several of the early church fathers state Peter was Mark's eyewitness and main source of information.

Mark was the first of the four gospel accounts to be written. It is thought that Mark wrote his account of Jesus' life for the Christians in Rome when they were experiencing great persecution around 64 A.D. Mark pointed to the long-awaited Davidic king and Messiah who came to earth as a servant. Just as Jesus suffered because of His servant attitude but ultimately triumphed, so too could the persecuted Christians in Rome. Mark's audience of Gentile believers may also explain why some elements seem to be missing from his gospel. These include fulfilled prophecy, references to the Law, and references to certain Jewish customs.

In the first half of his book, Mark focused on Jesus' service to others as He healed the sick, drove out demons, and ministered to the multitudes. In the second half of the book, Mark presented Jesus as the suffering servant whose focus narrowed to training the apostles as He journeyed to the cross and victory over death.

Mark 1

BACKGROUND

When Jesus was baptized, a voice from heaven announced His pleasure in His Son. This was one of three times God spoke from heaven about Jesus. The other two were the Transfiguration (Mk. 9.2-8) and the Triumphal Entry into Jerusalem (Jn. 12.27-30).

OVERVIEW

Mark began his record by using four terms that summed up what he would be writing. The Greek term translated *gospel* refers to the good news a messenger or herald would proclaim. *Jesus*, the earthly name of the Savior, means *Yahweh saves*. *Christ* is a Greek title meaning *anointed* and is a translation of the Hebrew word, Messiah. *Son of God* denotes Jesus' deity and unique relationship with God. Mark wrote, therefore, a proclamation of the good news of God's Savior, the long-awaited Messiah, and God's own Son.

Mark began by quoting from both Malachi (3.1) and Isaiah (40.3). The ancient societies relied upon oral communication much more heavily than in modern times. As a result, those quoting the Old Testament often assumed their listeners were so knowledgeable of the scriptures that they would not only recognize the passage but also understand the context from which it came.

Though the Holy Spirit would have resided in Jesus before He was baptized, being baptized was one means by which Jesus identified with sinful humanity. It also served to mark the beginning of Jesus' formal ministry as well as validate His divine identity.

It was customary to invite a visiting teacher to preach at the local synagogue. Jesus' teaching and command over the unclean spirits were surprising to those who listened because He did not rely on other teachers as was customary but showed that His authority came from Himself.

Mark included the detail that the sun had set before the people began to gather outside Simon's house to indicate the Sabbath had ended and, therefore, the people had not violated the Sabbath by carrying the sick to see Jesus.

Lepers were considered unclean members of society who were cast out of the community and avoided to prevent their disease and ritual uncleanness from spreading to other people. Jesus' compassion was active. He could have healed the man just by speaking. Instead, He also touched the leper, a repulsive act to anyone conscious of following the law.

The reason Jesus told the leper not to tell anyone is unclear. Possible explanations include: a desire not to prejudice the priest who had to declare him clean, a desire to avoid the reputation of being just a miracle worker, and not wanting to hasten the confrontation that was coming between Jesus and the religious leadership.

INSIGHTS

Jesus could easily have spent all His time healing the sick and casting out demons once word got out of His ability to do so. Instead of allowing all His time to be so filled, Jesus made a point of finding a place of solitude in which He could pray. Today, we too can be drawn into the constant needs that present themselves, needs that are often important and honorable to accomplish. Yet, we too must take times of solitude in which we can pray and reconnect with our Father. Just as with Elijah, God's voice is often still and small (1 Kgs 19.11-13), and it is often only in the quiet that we can really hear what He wants to say to us.

1. Do you follow Jesus' example to take time in solitude to connect with your heavenly Father? If not, what keeps you from doing so? How might you make solitude and prayer a more regular and meaningful part of your Christian walk?

2. When Jesus called the first disciples to follow Him, they left what they were doing and followed immediately. Think back to when you first heard the gospel message and Jesus calling you to follow Him. Did you respond immediately? Did it take you some time to follow? Are you still contemplating whether to follow Jesus? Consider how God pursued you in order that you would make a decision to follow. How does this convey God's love for you?

MARK 2

BACKGROUND

Tax collectors fell into two categories: those who collected the equivalent of an income tax and those who collected an excise or import tax on trade items. Since Capernaum was situated near important trade routes, it is likely import taxes were collected there. Even though such work was profitable, tax collectors were often viewed as collaborating with the Romans and therefore not well regarded. Many Jews did not associate with tax collectors of any type.

Levi was also called Matthew (Matt. 9.9).

OVERVIEW

Mats were often used as beds during this period, so it is possible that the friends were lowering the paralytic on a mat. Though Jesus acknowledged only the faith of the paralytic, his friends had to have faith as well in order to have been willing to lower their friend in the first place.

Blasphemy was defined as saying God's holy name or leading others away from God. In this sense, Jesus did not blaspheme. By Jesus' time, however, the scribes had broadened the definition to include doing or attempting to do those things that only God could do. While priests, acting as God's representatives, could pronounce forgiveness, both repentance and a sacrificial offering would have preceded the announcement. Jesus was not a priest, and the required offering had not been made, so in the eyes of the scribes, Jesus had done what only God could do.

When the scribes challenged Jesus under their breath, He challenged them openly. Indeed, anyone could *say* sins are forgiven, and there was no way of testing the statement's outcome. On the other hand, a pronouncement of healing could immediately be tested. The paralytic's ability to walk lent credibility to Jesus' forgiveness.

No one is righteous before God, so Jesus' statement is somewhat sarcastic. While He did come for sinners, it was not to condone their sins but to restore them to right relationship with His Father. That restoration requires repentance.

According to the Law of Moses, fasting was only required on the Day of Atonement. Religious groups, such as the Pharisees, had added additional occasions on which to fast. Fasting was viewed as an important part of prayer and penitence, so rabbis and their students often practiced it.

Wedding feasts were a time of celebration during which fasting, mourning, and difficult labor were not permitted. Jesus was not against fasting and used this analogy to explain why His disciples did not fast. There would come a time for fasting, mourning, and difficult labor, but for the moment, the disciples could enjoy the presence of their teacher.

Jesus' response to the Pharisees' accusation of working on the Sabbath did not directly address the innocence of either His disciples or David (1 Sam. 21.1-6). Rather, He pointed to the meaning of the Sabbath. God had intended that keeping the Sabbath was to be a blessing, not a burden. Because the Sabbath was made for humans and not humans made to observe the Sabbath, it was permissible to occasionally overrule the ceremonial observation of the Sabbath.

INSIGHTS

Levi, like the fishermen earlier, left a well-paying position in order to follow Jesus into an unknown and uncertain future. As we grow in our relationship with God, He may call us to forsake our comfortable, well paying, secure jobs for an unknown and uncertain future with Him. He asks us to follow in faith; trusting that He will provide what is needed when it is needed, not necessarily when we begin to feel uncomfortable. While we may enjoy the comfortable, secure job, we will never feel more fulfilled than when we do what God has called us to.

1. On his own, the paralytic would have had a very hard time getting through the crowds to seek healing from Jesus. It was only through the dedication and efforts of his friends that he was able to do so. Do you have one or two family members or friends for whom you would drop everything in order to help them when they need it? Are there people who would come to your aid if you called and said you needed help? God created us to live in fellowship and community with other people. If you don't have people you can call upon when you need assistance, what steps might you take in order to find a close friend or two?

2. The scribes and Pharisees were critical of the sinners Jesus chose to spend time with and critical of Jesus for spending time with sinners. Have you ever been drawn to help or minister to people your family and friends were critical of? What was your motivation for doing so? How can you extend Jesus' love and grace to people who are overlooked or forgotten?

Mark 3

BACKGROUND

Jews who supported Rome and especially the series of rulers named Herod (Herod the Great, Herod Antipas, etc.) were called Herodians. These supporters saw the ruling family as the last hope of maintaining Jewish nationalism as a distinguishable element in the Roman Empire. Because the Herodians supported Rome, they were generally bitter rivals of the Pharisees.

OVERVIEW

The Pharisees and other scholars continually debated what fell into the category of work and was, therefore, not permitted on the Sabbath. Although the debate was ongoing, compromises had been made in the area of saving a life and defending oneself. Minor illnesses that were not life-threatening had to wait until after the Sabbath had finished before receiving attention. This rule applied to physicians, though, and not to God. As a result, the Pharisees further debated whether it was lawful to pray for healing on the Sabbath.

Violations of the Sabbath were normally treated lightly with corporal punishment reserved for those who deliberately and purposefully violated the Sabbath. The Pharisees were motived by a desire to rid themselves of the threat Jesus presented and went beyond their normal traditions in trying to rationalize His death.

The Pharisees were willing to lay aside their differences with the Herodians in order to meet their common goal—the elimination of Jesus.

Jesus had a large following of disciples or learners. (Luke 10.1 states that Jesus appointed or sent out seventy others.) From His following, Jesus selected twelve with whom He would have closer contact and would train for certain leadership roles.

Having written his account of Jesus' life well after the events, Mark was able to state as fact what had not been apparent at the time: Judas, one of the called twelve, would eventually betray Jesus.

Beelzebub, meaning *Lord of the Flies*, was another name for Satan. While the assertion that Jesus used the power of Satan to cast out demons seemed logical to the scribes, it was not. Using demons to cast out demons was not a sustainable method of managing or obtaining power and would eventually lead to downfall, as Jesus pointed out.

There has been much debate about what *blasphemes against the Holy Spirit* means. Many believe that the sin is not one single act but an ongoing, to-the-point-of-death denial of God's presence and work in the world (one function of the Holy Spirit is to make these known).

INSIGHTS

The Pharisees *watched him [Jesus] closely* to see what He would do in the synagogue on the Sabbath. They were not interested in what Jesus had to say and what they might learn from Him, but only how they might entrap Him. Our hearts can become hardened to the message of Christ when we attend church with a hostile attitude, determined to find fault with what occurs. If we continually attend with these sorts of attitudes, we will miss the spiritual benefit and allow bitterness to settle in our souls. Nothing is perfect or perfectly pleasing to us. We need to allow for differences and focus on the spiritual message God would have us hear.

1. The Pharisees were so focused on the laws of the Sabbath, which defined what could and could not be done, that they lost sight of the reason for the Sabbath. Today we as a culture, in many ways, suffer from the opposite focus with the same effect. We do anything we like on the Sabbath and have also lost sight of the reason for the Sabbath. Why did God instruct humanity to observe a day of rest? (Gen. 2.1-3; Ex. 20.8-11) Is God calling you to be more intentional about observing the Sabbath? How might you adjust your focus and schedule to be more intentional about observing a day of rest and spending time with God?

2. Out of the many people following Jesus, He chose twelve to train and be close companions. Today we might call this a mentoring relationship. Do you actively look for people younger in their faith whom you can mentor? How might you share your life experiences and wisdom with others to encourage them in their own faith?

Mark 4

BACKGROUND

There are places in Palestine that form natural acoustic coves. At one such location near Capernaum, it is possible for up to seven thousand people to hear one person speaking from the center of the cove. Jesus' position in the boat on the lake facing the crowd likely had similar acoustical qualities that allowed a great multitude to hear Him[3].

OVERVIEW

Beginning with this chapter, Mark changed his focus from the works Jesus did to the words He spoke.

Seed was often sown in a field by scattering it in handfuls. It was not uncommon for some of the seed to fall on unprepared ground as well as the field.

The condition of the soil determined the quality of the plants that grew. Likewise, the condition of one's heart, whether Christian or non-Christian, determines what happens to the words of truth each person hears.

In very fertile regions of the Jordan Valley, it was possible to reach yields of a hundredfold. The average yield for Palestine was closer to tenfold. Regardless of the actual yield, the point was that the seed was worth sowing.

Jesus quoted from Isaiah (6.9-10) not to indicate that the parables He taught were beyond the understanding of most people or that they

[3] Craig S. Keener, *The IVP Bible Background Commentary: New Testament* (Accordance electronic ed. Downers Grove: InterVarsity Press, 1993)

contained a mysterious meaning that was known only to a select few but to point to the people's hardened hearts that refused to hear or heed the truth.

The *cares of this world* are akin to worry, while *deceitfulness of riches* and *desire for other things* corresponds to seeking after pleasure, often at the exclusion of higher priorities.

A life lived by hearing and accepting Jesus' truth will bear fruit in great abundance, just as seed sown in good soil will do the same.

Lamps were small clay bowls that were either pinched on one side to hold a wick or had a small hole into which the wick was inserted. The olive oil placed in the bowl provided the fuel the wick burned to produce light. Lamps were placed on stands so that they would illuminate as much area as possible.

Just as the purpose of a lamp was to bring light to dark places, so the purpose of Jesus' teachings was that they bring the light of truth to His listeners. Ultimately, Jesus wanted His teachings not just to be heard but applied as well.

The number of pagan rituals and sacrifices seeking divine help for harvesting a good crop attests to the belief that even pagans believed their gods, not man, were responsible for the grain growing. Jewish farmers sought God's provision through their crops with prayers and festival celebrations.

How a seed grew was not understood, yet it grew to bear fruit. In the same way, it is not understood how God's kingdom grows, but God is causing it to grow and bear its fruit.

With the parable of the mustard seed, Jesus pointed to the small beginnings His word would have and the great proportions to which it would grow.

As Mark told the story of the sudden windstorm on the Sea of Galilee, he related both Jesus' humanity and divinity. Jesus' need for sleep resulted from His human nature, while His command over the winds and the seas was a result of His divine nature.

INSIGHTS

There are many things, for example, how a seed stores enough energy to grow or what electricity is, that we do not understand. Not understanding, however, does not prevent us from trusting seeds will grow to produce food or lights will come on when we flip the switch. We also don't fully understand God—and never will, no matter how much knowledge we gain. Parts of God will *always* be a mystery. This lack of understanding should not stop us from trusting God. God *is* trustworthy. He will never forsake us (Deut. 31.6). In the darkest of moments, He is with us still.

1. Twice in this chapter, Jesus said that *anyone who had ears* should hear what He said. Why do you think Jesus phrased the instruction this way? Are you quick to hear what Jesus or fellow Christians have to say to you? Are you eager to incorporate all of Jesus' teachings into your life? Are there areas in which you prefer the light of Truth did not fall? How can you be one with ears that wholeheartedly hear and put into practice Jesus' message?

2. Why does Jesus liken the kingdom of heaven to the smallest of all seeds, the mustard seed? Though you may currently only have small faith, are you allowing God to grow it into great faith so that it may eventually bear much fruit for His kingdom? Are there things God might be calling you to do or to avoid so that your faith will grow? What fruit is currently being produced through your faith?

Mark 5

BACKGROUND

Decapolis, Greek for ten cities, was the name given to a region that represented ten Jewish cities that were primarily east of the Jordan and south of the Sea of Galilee. Pliny, the Greek historian, listed the cities as Damascus, Dion, Gadara, Gerasa (or Galasa), Hippos (or Hippo), Canatha (or Kanatha), Pella, Philadelphia (Rabbah or Rabbath Ammon in the Old Testament and today Amman, capital of Jordan), Raphana (or Rephana), and Scythopolis.[4]

OVERVIEW

People in several ancient cultures believed that spirits were most powerful at night. As a result, Mark's readers would continue reading with a sense of suspense as the conflict unfolded.

The spirit in the man living among the tombs had been tormenting the man for many years. It could not help but immediately recognize Jesus and came forward to worship Him, fulfilling Isaiah's prophecy that *to Me every knee will bow* (42.23).

In ancient times, it was believed that knowing a spirit's name was one means of gaining control over it. It was the common practice of ancient exorcists to attempt to identify spirits. Jesus, however, had no need to gain power over the spirits. This was the only time He inquired about a spirit's name, perhaps so those around Him would gain a greater appreciation for His power.

[4] Earl Radmacher, Ronald B. Allen, and H. Wayne House, editors, *Nelson's New Illustrated Bible Commentary* (Nashville: Thomas Nelson Publishers, 1995), 344-345

A legion in the Roman army consisted of between four and six thousand soldiers. The name indicated the man was hosting a large number of demons.

From the Jewish perspective, pigs were among the most unclean animals and would have been considered an appropriate place to send the spirits. The presence of the swine is an indication that Jesus was in Gentile country when this incident took place.

Though the demoniac had been healed, the people feared Jesus and wanted Him to leave. Their fear likely stemmed from two issues. First, the people had no ability to understood or comprehend the display of power they had just witnessed. Second, the drowned herd represented a significant economic loss. The people marveled at what Jesus had done but let fear get the best of them.

In previous instances when Jesus was in predominately Jewish areas where His Messiahship would have been easily misunderstood, He told those He healed not to tell anyone what had occurred. In this predominately Gentile area, however, the healing would have more likely been attributed to the powers of a magician. To combat this misperception, Jesus told the man to return home and tell his family and friends all that God had done for him.

Falling at the feet of another was done only in recognition of someone of great status, such as a king. When Jairus fell at Jesus' feet, he was paying significant tribute to Jesus' power and authority.

By Jewish law, a woman was unclean during her menstrual period. Anyone she touched would have been ceremonially unclean for the day and would have had to go through ritual purification.

The woman likely heard about Jesus' ability to heal and, not wanting to be embarrassed by her situation, had hoped to touch Jesus and then disappear into the crowd. Jesus was immediately aware of what had occurred and wanted to correct the woman's mistaken notion about what caused her healing. It was not the result of magical powers, but her faith and Jesus' divine will.

Because bodies decay quickly, mourners were called immediately upon the young girl's death.

That people would ridicule Jesus when He stated the girl was sleeping indicates there was no question in their minds that she had actually died.

INSIGHTS

While Jesus told the woman with the flow of blood that her faith had healed her, it is important to note that faith itself does not heal, nor is a certain amount of faith required. The woman's faith healed her because it was rightly placed in Jesus. Today, a sect of Christianity believes God heals everyone who has enough faith, that anyone who is not healed simply did not have enough faith. Nothing in scripture backs up this line of thought. Jesus often healed people with small and uncertain faith. Faith can prompt God to heal, but no amount of faith can guarantee healing.

1. Jesus told the man who had been freed from the unclean spirits to go home to his friends and tell them about all Jesus had done for him. How often do you share what Jesus has done for you with your friends? What things that Jesus has done might you share with others to encourage them in their own faith?

2. Jesus' awareness of being touched by the woman with the issue of blood indicates that not even the smallest of details escapes His notice. Are there any issues you are dealing with that seem too small to bring to Jesus? What do you think would happen if you invited Jesus into the smallest of details of your daily life? However small your faith, what needs can you lay at His feet?

3. The people ridiculed Jesus when He stated that the girl they knew to be dead was only sleeping. Have you ever faced ridicule when you have felt Jesus' prompting to do something that didn't make sense? How were you able to witness to those around you when what you were prompted to do came to pass? What effect did going through such an experience have on your faith?

MARK 6

BACKGROUND

Both Herod Antipas and his wife Herodias had a lust for power that eventually led to their downfall. Herod Antipas divorced his first wife in order to marry Herodias, the wife of his brother, Philip. King Aretas of the Nabataeans in Arabia, father of Herod's first wife, was insulted by the rejection of his daughter and found reason to attack Herod. Herod's loss was considered judgment for John the Baptist's murder. Herodias later convinced Herod to seek the title *king* from Rome. The request was opposed and Herod was condemned to permanent banishment.

OVERVIEW

Some scholars have suggested that the absence of Joseph's name when Jesus' brothers were listed indicates he had died by the time of Jesus' ministry. Of the four brothers listed, none were believers at the time of Jesus' crucifixion. James later became a believer and leader of the church in Jerusalem, as well as author of the New Testament book of James. Some have suggested that Jesus' brother, Judas, wrote the book of Jude, though no consensus has been reached.

Jesus encouraged the disciples to trust God for their provisions when He sent them out with only their staffs and sandals.

Oil is used throughout the Bible to symbolize God's blessing and healing. Those anointed with oil were often called to serve God (1 Sam 16.13). Though oil itself could not heal, it came to symbolize the pouring out of God's Spirit.

Mark took a break from his narrative to relate the death of John the

Baptist. Herod had enjoyed listening to John and was forced to murder John in order to keep from losing face before his guests. His murder of a man he perceived to be innocent was similar to Jesus' death at the hand of Pontius Pilate.

Herod would not likely have given half his kingdom to Herodias' daughter. This was thought to be a stock phrase that meant Herod would grant anything she asked.

Scriptures record several times when Jesus saw a need, was moved with compassion, and acted to fill the need. In this case, He was moved by the crowd's need for food despite an obvious lack of available food. Even if Jesus had sent the crowd out to find food for themselves as the apostles suggested, the local villages would have been hard pressed to feed over five thousand people on short notice.

Mark states five thousand men were fed. This did not include women and children who were also present (Matt 14.21, John 6.10).

The fourth watch of the night would have been between 3:00 and 6:00 a.m.

This account actually contains three miracles: Jesus was able to see the disciples in the dark miles from where He was, Jesus walked on water to the disciples, and He showed complete control over the powers of nature.

INSIGHTS

By sending the apostles out in twos, Jesus provided a pattern that can be followed today. Each member of the pair was able to support and encourage the other, as well as provide fellowship and accountability. Our culture is very individualistic and encourages us to rely on no one but ourselves. Scripture, however, tells us that two are better than one, with two able to do many things one cannot do alone (Ecc. 4.9-12). Though we may be tempted to "go it alone," ministering with others allows us to make the most of our God-given gifts as we live out Jesus' command to spread the good news to the ends of the earth.

1. Herod's promise to his stepdaughter did not turn out the way he intended when he was forced to kill John the Baptist in order to save face. Herod had the power to adjust his promise but was too concerned about how he would appear to those around him to actually do so. When have you put your image ahead of doing what is right? How can you adjust your priorities so that doing what is right is always more important than how you might look to others?

2. The disciples did not understand about the loaves because their hearts were hardened. Sometimes we are amazed at how Jesus works in the lives of those around us but refuse to believe He is willing or able to help us when we have needs. Where do you stand with Jesus? Do you take Him at His word and expect He will work in your life just as willingly as He works in other people's lives? Is there any bitterness, unbelief, or anger you hold against Jesus that you need to repent of and receive His forgiveness?

Mark 7

BACKGROUND

The Pharisees weren't the first to attempt to substitute ritual and tradition for true, heartfelt worship of God. Samuel rebuked Saul for offering sacrifices, which was one means of worshipping (1 Sam. 15.22), in place of obeying God. God warned His people that sacrifices and burnt offerings were no substitutes for knowing Him (Hos. 6.6).

OVERVIEW

The Pharisees practiced hand washing as a means of ensuring they were cleansed of any unintentional contact with unclean people, particularly in the marketplace. The ritual was not commanded in the Old Testament but was likely derived from the special washings priests practiced in order to purify themselves.

As a teacher, Jesus was responsible for the behavior of His disciples. As a result, the Pharisees questioned Jesus about the traditions His followers were not observing.

Jesus bypassed the Pharisees' question in order to address two issues of greater importance. First was the Pharisees' tendency to place greater significance on man-made traditions than the commands of God. Second was their practice of viewing ceremonial defilement as a greater offense than moral defilement.

Isaiah had prophesied against the nation of Israel of his day because they carried out religious rituals but did not seek after God's heart. Jesus quoted a portion of the prophecy (Is. 29.13) as an indication that the Pharisees were doing the same.

When the law was first given, the priests and other religious leaders would not write any commentary about it in fear they would wrongly influence succeeding generations. Over time, however, commentaries were written and collected in the Talmud. The Talmud was eventually viewed as having greater authority than the Torah (the Hebrew scriptures equivalent to the Christian Old Testament).

Corban was a Hebrew word meaning *devoted to God*. Once articles were devoted to God, they could not be used for any other purposes. Some people avoided supporting their elderly parents by placing their assets under such a vow.

Given all the laws and traditions about what was clean and unclean as well as how one became unclean, Jesus' assertion that nothing outside a man could make him unclean would have been a radical statement.

The woman who approached Jesus was a Gentile (indicated by the word *Greek*) and a native of the area. Syro-Phoenician indicated the Roman province of Syria and the ancient area of Phoenicia of which Tyre and Sidon were principle cities. It was located about fifty miles northeast of Capernaum in what is modern day Lebanon.

Jewish people viewed dogs as scavengers. Jesus was not insulting the woman by referring to dogs in His response. Rather, He was testing her faith. She understood His test and responded with persistence. In this manner, Jesus made clear that he did not heal by pagan magical powers but chose to heal because of the woman's demonstrated faith.

The healing of the deaf mute is one of two miracles recorded only by Mark. The other is the healing of a blind man (8.22-26).

INSIGHTS

Just as the Pharisees attempted to use external elements (what was eaten) to determine whether a person was defiled or not, so we often look to the things surrounding us as a means of placing blame. What is in a person's heart and mind leads to their thoughts and actions. Ultimately, each person must take responsibility for his or her own decisions. While it is easier to place the blame on someone or something else as both Eve and Adam did in the Garden (Gen. 3.9-13), God holds each person accountable for his or her own actions and judges each accordingly as He did in the Garden of Eden.

1. By following the *tradition of the elders,* the Jewish leadership put an unnecessary burden on themselves and the people to ensure they did nothing that would violate the Laws of Moses. They confused legalistic fulfillment of the law with worshipping God, who had given them the law to bring glory to Himself. Are there any rituals, rules, or even superstitions you practice in order to be good enough for God? Are you able to rest in God's love for you as you are without doing anything to earn His love? What changes might you need to make in order to worship God without any unnecessary burdens?

2. The Jewish people had long adhered to the dietary laws about which foods were clean and which were not. Jesus warned his disciples that it was not what people ate that made them clean or unclean, but what was in their hearts. What is in your heart? Do your thoughts, words, and deeds reflect a heart full of bitterness, anger, and hatred or God's love, peace, and joy? Even when our hearts are mostly godly, there can still be pockets of ungodliness. What changes might you need to make to remove any ungodliness from your heart? What might you do to better reflect God to those around you?

Mark 8

BACKGROUND

Caesarea Philippi was a city to the east and slightly north of Tyre. It was a pagan city known for its worship of Pan, a Greek nature god. Villages often developed around larger cities. The city was able to provide a degree of stability as well as the supplies the villages would otherwise lack.

OVERVIEW

Though the disciples had witnessed Jesus feed five thousand plus only a few days earlier, they still questioned how He would feed the four thousand currently with them.

The Greek word for the baskets used to collect the leftovers indicates a basket that was much larger than the baskets used in 6.43. This basket was similar to the one used to lower Paul over the wall in Damascus (Acts 9.25).

Jesus did not perform miracles to impress people, but to glorify His Father and draw people to faith in Him. The Pharisees' request for a *sign from heaven* was likely motived by a desire to test Jesus. They would already have seen many of the signs or miracles Jesus had performed. Those who doubted Jesus' divine authority would not be drawn to Him by a *miracle on demand.*

Jesus' caution to *beware of the leaven* was a warning against the growing corruption of both the Pharisees and Herod Antipas.

Despite the continued teaching the apostles received from Jesus, they were still slow to comprehend the meaning of what Jesus said.

The multi-stage healing of the blind man paralleled the apostles' perception of Jesus. They had begun to see, but could not yet clearly perceive all that Jesus said and did. Their *sight* was fully focused after the resurrection and coming of the Holy Spirit.

Messiah or *Christ* means *anointed one* and referred specifically to the descendant of David who would restore the kingdom of Israel. There were many different views of how the coming Messiah would reign. Although Peter confessed that Jesus was the expected Messiah or Christ, his view of how Jesus would reign (v. 32) was still quite different from the understanding he would gain after Jesus' death and resurrection.

Jesus gave the first of several predictions about His coming death. As Jesus revealed what was to come, He also began to teach and prepare His apostles for what they would endure on His behalf.

The cross was an instrument of torture and death used by the Romans. To take up the cross meant to carry the crossbeam.

Deny oneself did not refer to giving up something, but to giving complete control of one's life to Christ.

The temptation was to make the most of life on earth, but Jesus pointed to a different reality. Those who sacrificed on earth would experience eternal gain, while those who concentrated on earthly gain would experience eternal loss.

INSIGHTS

Though Peter was the first to state verbally Jesus was the expected Christ, he was also quick to rebuke Jesus for making predictions about His coming death. Peter had much to learn. In a similar manner, we can have preconceived notions about what God is up to or how He should be understood. We must be willing to learn all God has to teach us as well as have our misconceptions about God challenged and replaced by the truth. Just as Jesus was patient with Peter as he slowly learned the true nature of Jesus' identity and purpose on earth, so God is patient with us as we learn about Him and His calling on our lives.

1. The feeding of the four thousand came out of Jesus' compassion for the multitude. How often do you feel compassion for the needs of those around you? Do you ever go out of your way to help those in need? In what ways is Jesus leading you to have greater compassion for other people?

2. Jesus warned that whoever would strive to save their life would lose it, but whoever was willing to lose their life for Him would ultimately save it. What areas of your life have you not completely surrendered to Jesus? What areas are you attempting to control through your own power and efforts? How might you more fully surrender these areas to Jesus? In what ways can you ensure that Jesus will not be ashamed of you when you finally meet in heaven?

MARK 9

BACKGROUND

The last verses of the Old Testament mention both Moses and Elijah (Mal. 4.4-6). Moses is associated with the Law, central to the Jewish life, and Elijah was one of the first of the great prophets. God buried Moses (Deut. 34.5-6) and Elijah was taken up to heaven (2 Kgs 2.11).

OVERVIEW

Moses was the first to liberate God's people, and Elijah was viewed as one of the great prophets. Their presence with Jesus during His transfiguration served as a confirmation that Jesus was the Messiah Peter had confessed Him to be.

Peter's desire to build three tabernacles tended to put Jesus on the same level as Moses and Elijah.

The father had enough faith to bring his son to Jesus, but not enough to be convinced Jesus could heal his son. The father affirmed his faith in Jesus when asked, but also recognized his faith could be stronger than it was.

Some difficulties require preparation through prayer and fasting before being tackled. Fasting can help focus one's attention on God.

The apostles showed their continued lack of understanding about who Jesus was and what He was about when they debated who would be the greatest. Jesus' response pointed them away from the way the world judges and toward the way in which God esteems greatness. He also defined servanthood as the means of making a mark in God's kingdom.

Children in Jewish society were accorded very little status. The child Jesus picked up represented needy people. Most needy people were overlooked in favor of contact with those who had greater influence and power. Jesus called His apostles to humble themselves in service to the world and seek out those who were needy.

The ability to minister in Jesus' name came only from faith in Him in the first place. Those who did not believe in Jesus could not use His name to serve their own purposes. At the same time, God's work was not restricted to a select few but would be done by all who placed their faith in Jesus.

Stumble was used metaphorically to refer to sinning or falling away from faith in Christ.

Millstones were quite heavy and were used for grinding grain. Having a millstone tied around one's neck and thrown into a body of water would have led to drowning. Few worse fates existed in Jewish culture than to die without being buried.

Cutting off an arm or foot or cutting out an eye all were figurative for taking drastic action to avoid sin.

Seasoned with fire is believed to refer to the trials all people face. Believers face trials that purify their faith, while unbelievers face trials that encourage them to turn to God in faith.

Jesus ended this dialogue with a contrast to how it had started. He instructed His listeners to have peace with one another. He started the dialogue by inquiring about the dispute that had arisen among the apostles.

INSIGHTS

The father's response that he believed but needed help in his unbelief is a good statement for us today. God works in our lives as a result of our faith. Nowhere did Jesus say faith had to reach a certain level before He would perform a work of restoration. Instead, He looked for any faith, however small. The father acknowledged his faith and asked for help in growing and maturing that faith into something greater than it was. No matter how long any of us have been believers, there is always room for our faith to grow and mature as well. We too can ask God to help us in our unbelief.

1. The father's cry to Jesus that he believed but needed help with his unbelief seems like a contradiction. What was the father saying? Are there places in your own life where you believe but need help in believing? How can reading God's word help to bolster your belief? What other things is God inviting you to do in order to strengthen your belief?

2. In the world's value system, being first and winning are among the highest goals. Jesus turned this value system upside down when He stated that those who desire to be first need to be last and put others before themselves. Why do you think Jesus' values differ so greatly from the world's? Do you make a regular habit of serving others? How can you better serve one person today?

Mark 10

BACKGROUND

Under Jewish law, women were not permitted to divorce their husbands, but men were permitted to divorce their wives. The Law of Moses permitted husbands to write a certificate of divorce to their wives (Deut. 24.1-4). In Mark's Gospel, Jesus gave no exceptions when He prohibited divorce. Other New Testament references also prohibited divorce without exception (Lk. 16.18; Rom. 7.1-2; 1 Cor. 7.10-11). Matthew included an exception for sexual immorality (5.32; 19.9).

OVERVIEW

When they asked Jesus about divorce, the Pharisees may have wanted to see if Jesus would contradict the Law of Moses or offend Herod Antipas as John the Baptist had.

Jesus' question about the Law of Moses may have been motivated by a desire for the Pharisees to recognize the difference between what was commanded and what was permitted. God originally ordained marriage as a lifelong commitment between a man and woman. Moses, on the other hand, permitted divorce because of humanity's hardheartedness.

Jesus encouraged His followers to approach God's coming kingdom with the same qualities a child would: eagerness, sincerity, trust, and dependence.

Jesus quoted the seventh, sixth, eighth, ninth, and fifth commandments with the phrase *do not defraud* inserted just before the last commandment. These commandments had to do with human relationships and could be confirmed by witnesses (unlike the commandment not to covet, which focused on a heart issue).

Only one thing was necessary to inherit eternal life and that was faith in Jesus. The questioner admits he knows there is something more by stating he has kept the commandments. Jesus' response didn't suggest that some sort of work would get the man to heaven. Instead, Jesus was pointing the man to complete dependence on Him. Selling everything and following Jesus would leave the man with nothing but Jesus to rely upon.

A camel passing through the eye of a needle was hyperbole designed to highlight the impossibility of relying on anything but God's grace as a means of enjoying eternal life.

Leaving house, brothers, sisters, etc. did not mean renouncing them but rather making sacrifices for the sake of Jesus and the gospel.

Mark is the only gospel writer to mention that persecution as well as spiritual rewards would come to those who followed Jesus.

Drink the cup and *be baptized* were references to Jesus' coming persecution and death. James and John's agreement that they could do as Jesus stated was a greater commitment than either realized at the time. James would be the first apostle to be executed. John would be the last apostle to die but would witness the deaths of many Christians as well as suffer his own persecution and exile.

Jesus' life as a ransom meant it would serve as payment for those who were in bondage of one sort or another.

Jesus' followers viewed the blind man's pleas as an intrusion in their plans to establish Jesus' kingdom as soon as possible. They did not realize that the kingdom of God was all about such intrusions.

Bartimaeus was initially dissuaded from speaking out but quickly encouraged once he had Jesus' ear.

INSIGHTS

James and John were driven by personal ambition and desire when they asked to sit at Jesus' right and left hands. Jesus was quick to point out that true leadership in the coming kingdom resulted not from positions of power but from an attitude of service. To be great in Jesus' kingdom required taking on the lowliest of positions. Today, we too can be tempted to seek personal gain as we live our lives for Christ. Such motivation has no place in God's kingdom. As believers, God still desires that we take on the lowliest of positions—serving others—as we strive to become leaders in His Kingdom.

1. The disciples tried to keep the children from coming to Jesus, thinking they were too lowly for Jesus. Jesus rebuked the disciples and invited the children to come. Is there anyone you view as too lowly for your time and attention? What do you think Jesus would say to you about this? What would you say to Him? Why do you think Jesus said we need to receive the kingdom of heaven as little children in order to enter it?

2. If Jesus asked you the same question He asked Bartimaeus, namely, what do you want Jesus to do for you, how would you answer? What motivates do you have to ask this? Do you think Jesus would respond as He did to Bartimaeus, that your faith allows Him to grant your request? What, if anything, keeps you from having faith Jesus would answer your request?

Mark 11

BACKGROUND

The focus of Mark's gospel switches to the events of Passover week. These seven days, beginning with Jesus' triumphal entry into Jerusalem and ending with his resurrection, comprise roughly one-third of Mark's narrative.

Many have suggested that cursing the fig tree was an enacted parable that correlated to the spoken parable of the fruitless fig tree (Lk. 13.6-9). In both cases the fig tree represented Jerusalem, which was unresponsive to the message Jesus preached.

OVERVIEW

Bethany and Bethphage were just east of the Mount of Olives and about two miles from Jerusalem.

The crowd recognized Jesus and paid Him royal homage in three ways: laying clothing on the road (2 Kings 9.13), waving palm branches and laying them on the road, and repeating a messianic psalm (Ps. 118.25-26).

Hosanna means "save" or "save we pray."

The next day (v. 12) begins the events of Monday.

The buds of a fig tree were edible. Since the figs themselves would not be ripe for several months, Jesus was looking for the buds. An absence of buds by that time of year meant the tree would not produce fruit later in the season.

To a certain extent, the moneychangers in the temple were not doing anything they shouldn't have. Pilgrims traveling long distances had a difficult time carrying sacrifices on the journey and would have needed a place to obtain them. The pilgrims may also have come from locations where the currency was different from the standard used in the temple and would need a means of converting it. At issue were two items: the integrity with which the moneychangers were fulfilling the needs of the pilgrims and the amount of space they were using in the outer court. So much space was being used that Gentiles and those prohibited from entering further into the temple could not use the space to worship God as was originally intended.

In the morning (v. 20) begin the events of Tuesday. These events run together with those of Wednesday as the next day Mark recorded was *after two days* (14.1).

Casting a mountain into the sea was an impossibility that highlighted Jesus' point: what was impossible for man to accomplish was possible for God. Having faith was the key. Faith did not stop at believing God could and would do whatever was asked but extended into believing God would do those things that accomplished His will (1 Jn 5.14).

The temple authorities, in an effort to collect evidence against Jesus, inquired about the authority in which Jesus acted, specifically by which He had cleansed the temple. Jesus' question pointed to His authority to act and John's authority to baptize coming from the same source. The authorities understood the point of Jesus' question but were unwilling to allow such a possibility to be true.

INSIGHTS

Just as the moneychangers were able to justify their actions based on the needs of the visiting pilgrims, so it can be easy for us to justify less than righteous actions based on needs we see around us. Jesus was more concerned about attitudes of the heart. One test for whether what we are doing is righteous or not is to imagine standing before God and describing our activities. Would we be comfortable in such a conversation? What type of response would we imagine God giving? Would He praise us for our faithful use of His resources or rebuke us for misunderstanding His purposes?

1. Jesus got very angry with the moneychangers and those who bought and sold within the temple saying that His house of prayer had become a house of thieves. If Jesus were walking the earth today, where do you think He would have a similar reaction? God's dwelling place on earth was the temple. Paul tells us that our bodies are now the temple of God and His Spirit dwells in us (1 Cor. 3.16). Do you revere yourself as a temple of God and keep your temple as holy as Jesus wanted the temple kept holy in His day? If not, why not? What changes do you need to make to honor God in your temple?

2. Jesus told his disciples to forgive anything they were holding against others. If they chose not to forgive, they would not experience forgiveness by the Heavenly Father. How is your heart toward those who offend or wrong you? Are you quick to forgive? Forgiving someone does not mean what they did is OK, but that we release our right to vengeance and retribution to God. Do you agree or disagree with this statement? Why or why not?

Mark 12

BACKGROUND

Levirate marriage was a custom in which a man would marry his deceased brother's childless widow in order that she might have offspring. The practice was observed but not binding (Deut. 25.5-10).

A widow's mite was the smallest coin denomination of the time. It was worth only a few cents.

OVERVIEW

The parable of the tenants was a clear allusion to Israel. In the parable, the vineyard owner represented God. The vineyard was Israel. The tenants were the religious leaders who were to care for the nation. Those who were abused or killed by the tenants were the prophets God sent and whose messages had gone unheeded, and the owner's son was Jesus. In real life, landowners had great power and influence while tenant farmers had very little power. In the parable, the tenants act as if they have more power than they do and falsely believe that by doing away with the one who will inherit the land, they will put themselves in a position to inherit it.

Jesus was the chief cornerstone in God's plan for salvation (Ps. 118.22-23). His life, death, and resurrection are the foundations for all who are saved.

The Pharisees' question was a lose-lose proposition. A yes answer would alienate nationalistic Jews who opposed Roman rule while a no answer would indicate treason against the ruling government.

The Sadducees did not believe in the resurrection of the dead. Their question concerning the seven brothers and one wife was designed to make the concept of a resurrection appear absurd.

In response to the question about the greatest commandment, Jesus in effect summarized the Ten Commandments. Loving God with all one's ability was the essence of the first four commandments while loving neighbors well (as one would oneself) was the essence of the remaining six.

The only possibility for a descendant to be a superior to an ancestor was the one Jesus filled: both human (descendant of man) and God (Lord over all people).

Scribes were dependent on the generosity of the people for their support. Some, however, overstepped their bounds and took advantage of that generosity by demanding more than was appropriate or flaunting what they had instead of acting with humility and piety.

Jesus contrasted the offering of the wealthy with that of a widow. The wealthy contributed from their excess and in doing so did not sacrifice much. The widow, on the other hand, was poor and had little means of obtaining more than she had. She gave out of what she needed and trusted God to provide. Although the monetary amount the widow gave was much less than that of the wealthy, it was credited to her as more because of her sacrifice in giving it. In other words, the wealthy and widow were judged not on how much they gave, but on how much they kept for themselves.

INSIGHTS

The scribe who responded to Jesus understood better than most the spirit of the law. Most scribes of Jesus' day attempted to look good by offering the right sacrifices and doing the right things. This scribe understood that God looks not at what we do, but what we hold in our heart. Love toward God and those around us counts for far more than looking good on the outside. We would do well to come to the same understanding. Our efforts should be directed toward helping others and leading them to knowledge in Christ, not in feeding our own pride and ego.

1. What would it look like for you to wholeheartedly love God with your whole heart, soul, mind, and strength? How would your life look different? What areas might you be holding back from completely loving God? What prevents you from wholly surrendering yourself to God?

2. Why did Jesus say there were no commandments greater than loving God with our entire being and loving our neighbors as ourselves? If you don't love your neighbors well, is it possible to love God completely? What is one practical thing you could do today to better love those around you?

Mark 13

BACKGROUND

The temple structure consisted of several buildings and covered an area of approximately 20 acres. It was one of the most magnificent structures in the ancient world and highly prized by the Jewish people. Construction was begun by Herod the Great before Jesus' birth and continued after Herod's death. Completion of the structure is believed to have occurred just prior to 66 A.D. Construction would have occurred during Jesus' entire lifetime.

OVERVIEW

In this chapter, Mark relates Jesus' predications about the future. These dealt with the destruction of the temple, center of the Jewish world, as well as the end of the world. This speech is called the Olivet Discourse because Jesus gave it while sitting on the Mount of Olives.

For the disciples or anyone else for that matter, the thought of seeing the temple completely destroyed to the point of not one stone remaining on top of another would have been an astonishing thought.

Though Jesus was the true Messiah whom everyone was invited to believe in, He warned that many would come posing as the Messiah in an attempt to deceive and take advantage of people.

Four times in the course of this speech, Jesus warned his listeners to *take heed, watch out*, or *be on guard* (vs. 5, 9, 23, 33).

The general signs of the end times would include religious deception, fighting among the nations, earthquakes, famine, and suffering.

The *abomination of desolation* was a reference to the prophecies of Daniel and the destruction that would occur at the end of time (Dan. 11.31, 12.11). Josephus, a Jewish historian, believed the abomination of desolation took place in 66 A.D. when the blood of priests was shed in the temple. Others believed it took place when the Romans destroyed the temple in 70 A.D. If the phrase means the abomination that *caused* desolation, both dates could be accurate, with the events of 66 A.D. leading to those four years later.

Houses had flat roofs that were used for prayer, drying grain, etc. Access to the roof was from a stairway along the outside of the house. The admonition not to go into the house signified the haste with which one would have to flee; there would be no time to gather belongings from inside the house.

The phrase *to deceive, if possible, even the elect* indicates the failed attempt of the enemy to draw believers into the fray. Though believers must take heed, their faith in God means they will be shielded or protected by the power of God (1 Pet. 1.3-5).

The Son of Man was described in terms generally reserved for God and alluded to Daniel's reference of *one like* the Son of Man who would receive the kingdom from God (Dan. 7.13-14).

Jesus compared the coming astronomical signs to the growth of a fig tree. Both could be used to determine the season that was approaching.

Though many in the course of history have tried to foretell the moment of Jesus' return, none have been accurate. No future predictions will be accurate either as the moment is only God's to know.

Jesus' final parable in this discourse is unique to Mark. It warns that the servants should be vigilant at all times for the master's return because it could happen at any time and will happen without warning.

INSIGHTS

Predictions of the end times can cause great trepidation and apprehension. The trials and tribulations that will be experienced will cause great anguish and suffering. With God, however, there is always hope. For the believer, that hope is realized in the protection God will grant to all those who believe in His Son. This does not mean that believers will be free from experiencing *any* pain and suffering, but that they can anticipate the bright future of eternal life with God.

1. Jesus warned his listeners to take heed lest they be deceived. What was He encouraging them to heed? How can you guard against being deceived? Why is knowing and understanding scripture an important part of recognizing deception?

2. Though only the Father knows when the end times will come, we are to be prepared and vigilant for its coming. How do we prepare? Why does Jesus warn us to be vigilant? Why can we have hope in the tribulation and trials that will accompany the end times?

Mark 14

BACKGROUND

The bread and wine of the Passover meal represented deliverance from the bondage of slavery in Egypt. Jesus used the same bread and wine during the commemoration meal to broaden the definition of deliverance from bondage. Instead of slavery, people were now freed from the bondage of sin. Jesus became the perfect sacrificial Lamb required as part of the Passover meal. His death was symbolic of the killing of the lamb in the temple and His resurrection was victory over death that came as a result of sin (Gen. 2.17).

OVERVIEW

Fear of the crowd was a legitimate concern for the religious rulers in Jerusalem. During a festival celebration such as Passover, the population of the city could swell to five times that of normal times.

Alabaster was a translucent stone while spikenard was a perfume made from plants that grew high in the Himalayas and was imported from India.

One denarius represented a single day's wage of the average worker, so three hundred denarii was a substantial sum.

The Passover meal was to be eaten within the walls of Jerusalem (Deut. 16.16; *in the place He chooses* was where God chose to locate the temple).

Women nearly always carried the water jars, so a man carrying a water jar would have been conspicuous.

Jesus' statement that one of those eating with Him would betray Him may have brought to mind the prophecy of Psalm 41.9.

In Greek, the phrase, *Is it I?* is actually a negative question translated more accurately as *It is not I, is it?*

It was customary to sing songs of praise after the Passover meal. Traditionally songs from the Hallel, consisting of Psalms 113-118, would have been sung.

Jesus quoted from Zechariah 13.7 when He spoke of the sheep scattering after the shepherd had been struck.

Only Mark stated that the rooster would crow *twice,* not three times, to signify Peter's denials.

Abba was Aramaic for *papa*, a term used to show intimacy and respect. It could be used of one's own father or a teacher, but the Jewish people would not normally have used it when addressing God.

Jesus' arrest led to abandonment by His disciples, judgment by the religious leadership, and rejection by the people who less than a week earlier had heralded His arrival in Jerusalem.

Mark is the only writer to mention the young man fleeing naked. Some have speculated that it was a young Mark himself who had followed Jesus and then fled when caught.

The Sanhedrin was supposed to administer justice. Jewish law stated that two or more witnesses were needed in order to judge someone guilty. If the witnesses proved to be false because their testimony did not agree, the charges were to be dropped and the witnesses would suffer whatever penalty the accused would have suffered had s/he been found guilty (Deut.19.15-19). The Sanhedrin's determination to convict Jesus even after only false witnesses were produced shows the bias under which they were acting.

Under Jewish law, a person could not be convicted by his or her own testimony.

The curses Peter uttered would not have been vulgar words. Rather he would have invoked curses upon himself if he was not who he said he was.

INSIGHTS

When Peter said he would not abandon Jesus, he firmly believed what he said. When the time came to act upon those words, however, Peter lost his courage and denied not once, but three times that he knew Jesus. Likewise, we may imagine how we will respond in times of trial and then find our actual response is far from desirable; even showing the cowardice and fear of Peter's denials. While God would choose for us to stand in righteousness, He nevertheless understands the weaknesses of the flesh. Just as Peter later became a leader in the church, so God can also use us to do great works even after we have failed Him.

1. Jesus prayed that the cup of suffering He was about to experience would be taken away if the Father willed. What trial or suffering have you prayed God would take away, but He allowed you to endure? What did you learn about God through the experience? What did you learn about yourself? How would you encourage someone going through his or her own difficult trial?

2. The high priest, chief priests, elders, and scribes were not able to accept who Jesus said He was because they had preconceptions and assumptions about the Messiah that were not true. What preconceptions or assumptions might be getting in your way of fully understanding Jesus and the gospel message He delivered? How can you replace these with the truth?

Mark 15

BACKGROUND

Though Mark does not state that events in this chapter specifically fulfilled prophecy, several instances are included. The soldiers casting lots and dividing Jesus' clothing was prophesied in Psalm 22.18. Jesus' cry just before dying is the opening verse of Psalm 22. Dying amidst other criminals was predicted in Isaiah 53.12.

OVERVIEW

The Jewish leaders did not have the authority to execute anyone, so they prepared Jesus to go before Pontius Pilate, governor of Judea. The leaders hoped Jesus' claim of Messiahship would be seen as a threat to the governing powers and lead to a charge of sedition and treason against the emperor.

Mark paused in order to relay the custom of releasing a prisoner during a feast and included details about Barabbas. He is the only writer to note that Barabbas was part of a group of rebels who had committed murder.

Pilate knew the charges against Jesus were inconsequential and attempted to release Him. Pilate, however, succumbed to the will of the crowd by releasing Barabbas and condemning Jesus to death. Crucifixion was the most agonizing of executions practiced in antiquity.

The Praetorium was the governor's official residence. Pilate lived in Caesarea and would have used the palace only when visiting Jerusalem.

The purple robe and the crown of thrones were intended to mock Jesus and His claim to be deity.

Mark is the only gospel writer to identify Simon of Cyrene as the father of Alexander and Rufus. Cyrene contained a large Jewish settlement and was located in current day Libya.

The drink of wine and myrrh is believed to dull pain and was given to those about to be executed.

Hours of the day were measured from sunrise. So the third hour would have been from approximately 8:30-9:30 am at that time of year.

A stone inscription found in Caesarea, which mentions Pontius Pilate, prefect of Judea. Personal photo

Asphyxiation was usually the cause of death from crucifixion. It often took days to occur, so Jesus' death after just a few hours of suffering was unusual.

The Holy of Holies was separated from the rest of the temple area by a curtain or veil (Ex. 26.33). The rending of the veil signified that Christ's death achieved accessibility to God for all believers apart from the temple. The old covenant was no longer in effect as the new covenant instituted by Jesus had taken its place.

Mark records the irony of Jesus' death when only a Gentile soldier recognized that Jesus was who He claimed to be.

The council of which Joseph of Arimathea was a member would have been the Sanhedrin. Asking for the body of Jesus was a courageous act as it would have set Joseph in direct opposition to the Sanhedrin and identified him as one of Jesus' followers.

INSIGHTS

The chief priests and scribes mockingly told Jesus that if He would come down off the cross they would believe in Him. Their claim was unfounded, as they had seen many miracles Jesus had performed and chosen not to believe. Likewise, we can see the works of God in our midst and still choose not to believe. A sinful heart convicted of the need for the salvation Jesus offers most often motivates belief. Short of such a conviction, it can be easy to believe that any needs we have can be fulfilled through human effort.

1. How is it that in less than a week, the crowds could go from honoring Jesus with their praises to shouting for His crucifixion? Are you easily swayed by what other people say and do? How can you guard against being unduly influenced by those around you?

2. Pontius Pilate was more interested in gratifying the people than he was in acting upon the truth. Are there any areas of your life in which you have compromised the truth in order to gratify other people? What would it take to bring integrity to this area? Who might you enlist to help you live a more godly life?

3. Joseph of Arimathea acted with great courage when he asked for Jesus' body. In what areas of your life is God leading you to act with great courage? In what ways do you sense God bolstering your courage?

Mark 16

BACKGROUND

The great commission to go into all the world and preach the good news to all creation is contained in all four of the Gospels (Matt. 28.19; Mk. 16.15; Lk. 24.47; Jn. 20.21). Jesus came to earth to start a work but not to complete it. Completion was left with those who followed; first Jesus' apostles and disciples, then those who followed in belief in Jesus' saving grace and compassionate forgiveness that allows restored relationship with the Heavenly Father.

OVERVIEW

Before a body was buried, it was generally anointed with oil and then rinsed with water. Because Jesus' body had been taken down so close to the start of the Sabbath, there had not been time to properly prepare it for burial. As a result, the women went to the tomb with the spices to do what they had been unable to do at the time the body was laid in the tomb.

The sun would have risen at about 6:30 a.m. at that time of year. Some merchants would have already been out selling their wares, allowing the women to stop and buy spices before going to the tomb.

In ancient Jewish literature, angels often wore white. The women likely did not automatically assume the presence in the tomb was an angel as many priests and temple workers also wore white.

After many of the miracles Jesus performed, the recipient was instructed to go and tell no one. That instruction was often ignored as the recipient spread the news of what had occurred. Here, the women were instructed to go and tell the disciples, but they kept silent out of fear. Eventually, they gave voice to what they had witnessed.

The specific mention of Peter indicates his acceptance by Jesus, even though he had denied knowledge of Jesus two days earlier.

Two of the oldest surviving manuscripts of the Gospel of Mark end after verse 8. The abrupt ending matches the abrupt beginning and may well represent the original writings of Mark. Some argue, however, that verses 9-20 were part of the original writings and they are recognized as part of the Gospel by some of the earliest church fathers.

Though the women had seen the empty tomb and been told of Jesus' resurrection, they had not actually seen Him. Only after He appeared to Mary Magdalene was there an eyewitness to His resurrection.

The witness of women was not considered reliable, so it is not surprising that the testimony of Mary Magdalene was not believed.

Five signs were to accompany belief placed in Christ. Three of those signs were manifest in the early church: casting out demons (Acts 16.18), speaking in new tongues (i.e. known languages, Acts 2.4-11), and healing the sick (Acts 28.8). The other two, handling serpents and drinking anything deadly, are not attested to anywhere in early church writings.

Jesus' assentation into heaven to sit at the right hand of God served as confirmation that he was the Son of God. A ruler's right hand represented his power and authority, so Jesus' position at God's right hand was a testimony to all He had said and done on earth.

INSIGHTS

Once they fully understood Jesus' message, the disciples readily went into all the world to preach the good news. We too, as co-believers in Jesus Christ, are commissioned to spread that same good news. How that commissioning manifests itself in each believer varies. Some are called to travel to distant countries as missionaries. Some are called to use their resources in support of foreign and local efforts to spread the gospel message. Others are called to spread the word to those with whom they work and associate. Our obedience to God's individual call will help ensure that all the world hears the good news.

1. The women initially did not say anything, fearing the disciples would consider their testimony outrageous. When has fear caused you to keep silent when you should have spoken up? How can you overcome fear so that you can speak as God directs? John wrote that perfect love casts out fear (1 Jn. 4.18). How can this truth help you overcome fear?

2. Having watched Jesus die, it is understandable that the disciples did not believe Mary Magdalene when she reported she had seen the risen Jesus. Though their reaction was understandable, it did not change the fact that what she had seen was true. How quick are you to respond to the truth of Jesus? Do you willingly and eagerly share the good news of the risen Christ with those who need to hear? If you are not, what keeps you from doing so? What is one practical step you could take to be more generous with the good news?

LUKE

The same author wrote Luke and Acts. Little is known of the writer, and what is known comes primarily from three New Testament sources. Paul, the writer of thirteen epistles (or letters), referred to Luke as *the beloved physician* (Col. 4.14). He listed Luke among co-workers sending their greetings and included him separately from the Jews *who are of the circumcision* (Col. 4.11), leading some to believe Luke was a Gentile. If this were true, Luke would be the only Gentile author of a Biblical book. Luke was a *fellow laborer* (Philem. 24) and remained a close companion throughout Paul's ministry. Towards the end of his life, Paul wrote to Timothy, "Only Luke is with me" (2 Tim. 4.11).

Luke's account of Jesus' life was initially written specifically to Theophilus of whom little is known, though it appears to have a broader appeal to all people. The letter's purpose was to provide Theophilus with *the certainty of those things in which you were instructed*. Luke was methodical in his approach to the events and interviewed *eyewitnesses and ministers of the word* (Luke 1.2-4). He also used other sources, including the Gospel of Mark, and recorded many events not found in the other gospels.

Luke focused on Jesus' humanity more than any other gospel writer. In Luke's account, Jesus entered fully into the human condition and, as a result, suffered betrayal, loneliness, abuse, humiliation, and abandonment. Though fully God, this portrayal of Jesus' humanness has allowed many people throughout history, including the present day, to identify more fully with Him.

Luke also took great pains to present Jesus' love for people. The focus is not only on those who were naturally lovable but included the Romans and Samaritans, women and prostitutes, sick and crippled, slaves and thieves, and all those treated as second-class citizens or despised by the common Jewish community and religious leaders. Due to this focus, there are several accounts recorded only in Luke. These include the Good Samaritan (10.25-37), healing the crippled woman

(13.10-17), healing the ten lepers (17.11-19) and healing the high priest's servant (22.50-51).

Like the rest of the Bible, Luke's account of Jesus' life has great application to our lives today. What Jesus did for the countless people of His time, He longs to do for us today. As it did then, this gospel points to the richness of life we gain by having faith in a Messiah who is both fully man and fully God, able to give sin-filled lives meaning, mighty enough to redeem the most heinous of abuses, yet tender enough to walk with us through the most heartbreaking moments of our lives. He is a Savior worth knowing!

Luke 1

BACKGROUND

Herod the Great was king of Judea from 37 to 4 B.C.

Zacharias' and Elizabeth's righteousness before the Lord and experience of childlessness into old age would have caused contemporary readers to think of Abraham and Sarah, who experienced similar circumstances (Gen. 17-18).

Gabriel is one of two named angels in the Bible; Michael is the other (Dan. 10.13, 12.1).

Circumcision was the sign instituted by God to mark the covenant He had made with His chosen people (Gen. 17.10-14).

OVERVIEW

Theophilus, although a Greek in origin, was a common name among the Jewish people of the time. The title Luke used, *most excellent*, may have been a literal title indicating Theophilus' position in the upper class of Roman society, though it is also possible that Luke used it as a courtesy title.

The birth of John the Baptist appears only in Luke's gospel.

It was commonly believed that being barren was judgment for past sin. As Luke introduced Zechariah and Elizabeth, he was careful to point out that they were righteous before God and, therefore, the childlessness they experienced was not judgment for past sin.

Priests served in the Temple for two one-week periods each year. It is thought there could have been as many as 18,000 priests and Levites available to perform these Temple duties. As a result, casting lots was often used to make assignments to members of specific orders or divisions within the priests and Levites. A priest was given the honor of offering incense only once in his lifetime.

Zacharias' duties encompassed throwing incense on the burning altar of incense and would not have taken very much time. His delay caused the crowd to worry. If his offering had not been accepted, their prayers would have been in jeopardy.

The virgin conception pointed to the birth of someone who was special and different from the rest of humanity.

The Old Testament form of the name *Jesus* is *Yeshua* or *Joshua* and means *Yahweh is salvation*.

The law required that circumcision be performed on the eighth day after a son's birth, which was often accompanied by much celebration by the surrounding community.

Both Mary's and Zacharias' songs of praise are filled with Old Testament references and echo Old Testament events. For instance, compare Mary's song with Hannah's in 1 Samuel 2.1-10.

INSIGHTS

Mary's response to the angel's announcement was humble acceptance. She did not understand how all that was announced would occur or why she among all other women was chosen, but she responded to God as a humble servant. In doing so, Mary serves as a model for our response to God's call on our own lives. Though His task may seem impossible and we may not understand how He will cause all He proclaims to come to pass, we will experience great blessings by choosing to respond humbly as His servant.

1. In what ways is God calling you to serve Him? How have you responded when the task God is calling you to perform seems beyond your ability? How can you more fully and confidently rely upon God in the midst of humbly accepting what He has called you to?

2. Both Zechariah and Mary responded to the angel Gabriel with virtually the same question—how. Why do you think Gabriel responded differently to the two questions? What do the questions indicate about where Zechariah's and Mary's hearts were as they contemplated what Gabriel was telling them? Where is your heart when you hear God speak to you?

Luke 2

BACKGROUND

The Law of Moses decreed that all firstborns were to be consecrated to the Lord and redeemed (Ex. 13.2, 12-13). After giving birth, a woman would complete a period of forty days (male child) or eighty days (female child) purification, then offer a lamb as a burnt offering and a turtledove or pigeon as a sin offering. A turtledove or pigeon could be substituted for the lamb if the family was poor (Lev. 12).

OVERVIEW

Censuses were conducted on a somewhat regular basis in order to appraise taxes. It is likely Joseph had to return to Bethlehem not because that was where he was born, but because he had never changed his registration to Nazareth or because he still owned property in Bethlehem.

Most tax laws in the Roman Empire required only the head of the household to appear, making Mary's journey unnecessary. Joseph may have felt uncomfortable leaving a very pregnant Mary alone while he traveled to Bethlehem. He may also have been aware that the circumstances surrounding Mary's pregnancy left her with little support from family and friends should she give birth while he was away.

It was believed that an infant's limbs had to be kept straight after birth in order to grow properly. *Swaddling clothes* were long strips of fabric wrapped around the baby to accomplish this.

Religious people often despised shepherds because their work kept them from participating in many religious functions. They were also ceremonially unclean on a fairly regular basis, and their testimony was not permitted in a court of law because they were considered untrustworthy. As a result, the angels' appearance to shepherds would have challenged the religious community.

Multitude of heavenly hosts indicates a number too great to count.

The two turtledoves or pigeons offered by Mary indicate that the family was poor and emphasizes the lowly status from which Jesus began His life on earth (Lev. 12.8).

The consolation of Israel referred to the Jewish hope in a Messiah who would deliver the people from political bondage to other nations.

Simeon recognized Jesus as the long awaited Messiah not only for the Jewish people but also the Gentiles as prophesied in the Old Testament (Is. 49.6).

All Jews were called on to make an annual pilgrimage to Jerusalem for the Passover (Deut. 16.5-6), though many did not due to the distance involved. Assuming a caravan traveled an average of twenty miles per day, the journey from Nazareth to Jerusalem would have taken approximately three days.

Luke is the only Gospel writer to record anything about Jesus' childhood.

INSIGHTS

Joseph and Mary did not fully understand Jesus' mission or purpose for His earthly presence. The disciples would experience similar difficulties as they grew in their knowledge and understanding of Jesus' mission. On the other hand, Simeon and Anna understood immediately who Jesus was when they saw Him. Similarly today, some who hear the good news understand immediately the significance of the salvation Jesus offers, while others struggle for years to understand. However, God promises that all who seek Him with all their heart *will* find Him (Jer. 29.13).

1. The angels' appearance to the shepherds sets the tone for the beginning of Jesus' life on earth. Jesus would regularly have compassion on and take time to be with the underprivileged and despised. How do you respond when someone less privileged or even despised crosses your path? Do you extend dignity to a fellow human being and do your interactions reflect a lack of compassion and respect? How can you move toward extending the same love and grace of the Father to all people regardless of who they are?

2. Both Simeon and Anna had been promised they would see the world's Savior before dying. Both lived their long lives in hope and rejoiced when their promises were fulfilled. Do you live in the hope that God's promises to you will be fulfilled, even if the fulfillment seems to be long in coming? How does knowing God is a promise-keeping God help or hinder you as you face trials and suffering?

Luke 3

BACKGROUND

Genealogies for Jesus are recorded in both Luke and Matthew, though there are differences between the two. Scholars have offered various explanations regarding these differences, with the most prominent being:

- Matthew likely records Joseph's genealogy, while Luke likely records Mary's;
- Luke records a more literal genealogy, while Matthew's is more spiritual;
- Levirate marriages (Deut. 25.5-10) may be included in one and not the other.

OVERVIEW

For the Jews, salvation was achieved by being born into a Jewish family (as evidenced by claiming to be a descendant of Abraham) and not rejecting God's laws. Any Gentile (non-Jew) could experience the same salvation by converting to Judaism. John the Baptist called *all* people to repent in order to experience salvation. He baptized those who repented as a sign of that salvation. Such a suggestion would likely have been offensive to the Jewish religious leaders.

A viper was a venomous snake. The young of a viper were believed to eat their way out of their mother's womb. Calling the crowd a *brood of vipers* was, therefore, a great insult by John.

Most people had one tunic and just enough food to get by. Those who had more were considered well off. Both tax collectors and soldiers were in positions to take advantage of people for their own benefit. Luke highlighted these three groups of people to indicate the heart change that was needed to truly live a life pleasing to God.

Winnowing was a process of separating grain from chaff (the husk of the grain). It was done after the grain had been threshed or separated from the plant stalk. In John's day, the grain was piled on a threshing floor (a covered area with open sides which allowed the wind to blow through) and a pitchfork type tool was used to throw the grain in the air, allowing the lighter chaff to blow away. John used this imagery to illustrate the separation that would take place between the righteous and the wicked.

What shall we/I do in order to achieve salvation is a theme repeated throughout Luke as well as Acts.

Luke's genealogy traced Jesus' ancestors all the way back to Adam. As the *son of Adam*, Jesus was a real human, while as the son of David, He was the Messiah.

INSIGHTS

One of the great mysteries regarding Jesus is His nature as fully man and fully God. Much debate has occurred over the centuries as to how this can be and what it means. And though the debate will go on until Jesus' second coming, we can take comfort in the realization that He is both man and God. Jesus' human nature means there is nothing we experience during our lifetimes that Jesus cannot fully relate to on human terms. His divine nature means that as part of the Godhead there is nothing beyond His ability or control.

1. John the Baptist was the forerunner to Jesus, sent to declare His imminent arrival. Why do you think God sent John instead of just sending Jesus? Who served as the forerunner to Jesus in your faith walk by preparing the way for Jesus to come? In whose life are you able to prepare the way for Jesus by proclaiming His truth? How has God made crooked paths straight in your life?

2. As people heard John's message of repentance, they began to wonder if John himself might be the Christ. He was quick to set them straight about who he was and who they should be expecting. How quick are you to point people to Jesus when people give you credit for what rightly belongs to Jesus? When you engage in ministry and serving others, do you do it with the same heart John did to prepare the way for Jesus?

Luke 4

BACKGROUND

Though Jesus was said to open and later close the book from which He read in the synagogue, He would actually have unrolled and read from a scroll rather than a book as we know it today.

God sent famine as judgment on the unfaithful nation of Israel. During that time only two Gentiles, the widow at Zarephath and Naaman the Syrian, received healing (1 Kgs. 17.8-24; 2 Kgs. 5).

OVERVIEW

Satan tried three times to entice Jesus to bow to his authority. Each time, Jesus quoted scripture to repudiate Satan's temptations. In the first temptation, Satan challenged Jesus' identity and authority. In response, Jesus quoted Deuteronomy 8.3 and declared His dependence on God. Since the Spirit had led Jesus into the wilderness for a time of fasting and preparation for ministry, eating at Satan's direction would have shown a lack of dependence on God. In the second temptation, Satan offered Jesus power through the wrong means. In making the offer, Satan exaggerated his own power. He has great influence over and ability to sway events in the world, but this does not include the ability to direct kingdoms as he chooses. Jesus responded by quoting Deuteronomy 6.13 and 10.20, thereby recognizing that only God is worthy to be worshipped and served. Satan's third temptation was an attempt to test the reliability of the scriptures. Satan's quotation of Psalm 91.11-12 was taken out of context and misrepresented God's will. Jesus responded by quoting Deuteronomy 6.16, which referred to an incident in Israel's history when they chose to test God instead of trust Him. Jesus would not repeat the nation's earlier lack of trust.

In the synagogue, Jesus read from Isaiah 61.1-2a. Though Luke had not yet relayed any miraculous incidents, Jesus would do all the things described in the passage. *The acceptable year of the Lord* was an allusion to the Year of Jubilee in which debts were canceled, slaves were freed, and ancestral lands were returned to their original owners. Jesus' focus was on freedom from spiritual bondage, which could be attained by belief in Him.

Simon's mother-in-law's healing was instant as attested to by the fact that she immediately began serving her guests.

The unclean spirits recognized Jesus and gave testimony to who He was. Why Jesus silenced them is not stated, though speculations include: Jesus did not want His role as Messiah revealed by demons, it was not yet God's time to reveal Jesus' identity, and Jesus wanted His works to give testimony to His identity.

The irony of Jesus' reference to Elijah revolves around the prophet's rejection by the Jewish king and acceptance by a Gentile woman. Jesus, too, would be rejected by many Jewish people and embraced by many Gentiles.

After ministering to the crowds, Jesus sought a deserted place.

INSIGHTS

Both Elijah's and Elisha's rejection by the king of Israel led to a time when the unlikely Gentiles, the widow at Zarephath and Naaman, saw God's mighty hand at work because of their faith. Their attitude often reflects attitudes we may find today: those we think will respond positively to God's message of redemption do not, while those we view as unlikely to respond do. It is essential that we not prejudge, especially concerning those we think might not believe. Our role is to fulfill God's plan by sharing His Good News with anyone and everyone to whom God directs us. We will not be held accountable for how someone responds, only for delivering the message.

1. Jesus repeatedly removed Himself from the activities of life to spend quiet time in solitude and prayer. How often do you seek places of solitude in order to connect with God in prayer? What, if anything, stops you from doing this? How can you make solitude and prayer a more regular and meaningful part of your spiritual life?

2. Each time Satan tried to tempt Jesus with a lie, He refuted it with truth. Are you able to recognize when you are being tempted with a lie? How often do you turn to scripture in order to refute a lie and be encouraged by the truth? What are some ways you might become more familiar with scripture in order to lean on truth in the midst of temptation?

Luke 5

BACKGROUND

The Lake of Gennesaret is also known as the Sea of Galilee and Sea of Tiberias.

Palestinian houses were usually one story and included an outside stairway that allowed easy access to the roof.

The Pharisees were a religious and political party known for their commitment to the law and maintaining ritual purity. Teachers of the law, also known as scribes, were trained in the Law of Moses.

OVERVIEW

The shore would have provided the same acoustical advantage as an amphitheater, so using a boat to withdraw somewhat from shore would have made Jesus easier to hear.

Nighttime, considered the best time to catch fish, had failed to produce a catch. Peter showed a high level of trust in a man he had only recently met. Fishermen would likely have shown such trust in a rabbi in spiritual matters but would have been less likely in matters related to their own expertise.

The income made by fishermen tended to be better than average. Forsaking such a lucrative career in order to follow Jesus included a radical economic change.

People regarded lepers as outcasts and generally avoided all contact with them. Jesus' willingness to touch a man with leprosy is evidence of His compassion toward those who suffered.

By sending the healed man to the Temple to be examined by a priest and make an offering, Jesus was complying with the law handed from God to Moses (Lev 14.1-32).

By Jewish definition, blasphemy consisted of speaking God's name or encouraging people to follow pagan gods. Jesus did neither when he forgave the sins of the paralytic. It was common belief that only God could forgive sins, so the scribes and Pharisees were focusing on Jesus' apparent audacity to do what only God could do.

Because tax collectors collected for the Roman Empire, they were viewed as collaborating with the enemy and were generally despised, especially by the Jewish religious leaders. Many believed that sharing a meal with a sinner was akin to accepting that person's sin. For the Pharisees, it was unthinkable that any prophet or learned religious man would associate with such disdained members of society.

Jesus compared his presence to that of a bridegroom. During the joyful wedding celebration, which lasted for seven days, guests were not permitted to fast, engage in any acts of mourning, or participate in any heavy labor. Jesus gave the first hint of His coming death by referring to the removal of the bridegroom.

Patching old clothing with new cloth would often cause the old clothing to rip as the two pieces of cloth shrank unevenly. New wine was not poured into old wineskins because the new wine expanded as it fermented. Old wineskins were already stretched from the previous wine and would have ripped under the pressure of the expanding wine. Both of these parables alluded to the conflict that occurred between the old ways (Judaism) and the new ways Jesus was teaching.

INSIGHTS

Peter's response to the miracle Jesus performed was to recognize his own unworthiness. Jesus responded with reassurance, *do not be afraid*, and a call to participate in His ministry, *from now on you will catch men.* Jesus continues to do for us what He did for Peter, namely to reconcile us with God as we repent of our sins. He also gives us the same opportunity He gave Peter, to go out and rescue people from the danger and condemnation of sin.

1. The man with leprosy was healed because he asked Jesus to do what he fully believed Jesus could do. How would you rate the level of your belief that Jesus can heal? Are there anything physical, spiritual, or emotional wounds you need to ask Jesus to heal? How can you address anything that keeps you from asking?

2. The Pharisees regularly judged Jesus without fully understanding who Jesus was. How can you make sure your ideas of who Jesus is are correct? If God reveals some of your beliefs are not fully accurate, is your heart open to revising them? Do you weigh what you think against what scripture says?

LUKE 6

BACKGROUND

Disciples were those who chose to follow Jesus. They learned as Jesus directed His teachings to the crowds in general and specifically to the disciples. The apostles were the twelve disciples specifically called by Jesus to be His representatives. The apostles spent more time with Jesus and later became the initial leaders of the church after Jesus' death, resurrection, and ascension.

OVERVIEW

Plucking, rubbing, and eating grain was akin to reaping, threshing, and preparing food, which the Pharisees viewed as a violation of the commandment not to work on the Sabbath. In response, Jesus claimed two things. First, the disciples were doing no differently than David when he used the showbread to satisfy the hunger of his men and himself (1 Sam. 21.3-6). Second, Jesus himself had authority over the Sabbath and that authority put Him in a position to state what honored God and what did not. The Pharisees' strict adherence to the letter of the law while ignoring its intent repeatedly clashed with Jesus' teachings.

When Jesus healed the man with the withered hand, He once again adhered to the Sabbath laws. Although the religious leaders were filled with rage, there was nothing unlawful about asking another to stretch out his hand.

The names of the apostles were all common names of the day. The differences found between Luke, Matthew (10.2-4), and Mark (3.13-19) may result from nicknames or secondary names being used in one or other of the lists.

Luke's *Sermon on the Plains*, though shorter, is very similar to Matthew's *Sermon on the Mount* (Matt 5-7). It has been suggested that Luke recorded a shorter version of the same sermon or that Jesus presented the teaching on multiple occasions, with Luke recording a different presentation than Matthew.

Blessed means divine favor and protection that results from experiencing God's grace.

Conventional wisdom of the times held that God's blessing or lack of blessing in a person's life was evident by the material wealth and influence s/he enjoyed. Jesus' teaching pointed to a reality that didn't use material wealth as a sign of God's blessings. Material things last only temporarily, while a person's character has eternal significance.

In contrast to the blessings that result from obedience to God's laws, Jesus also presented *woes* or curses that would befall those who neglected God and His laws.

Jesus was not condemning those who were rich, ate plenty, enjoyed life, or had a good reputation. Rather, He was condemning those with selfish and self-righteous heart attitudes that were ungrateful and didn't care for those who were disadvantaged. It was (is!) easy to pursue the rich life at the neglect of the godly life.

Jesus' teaching, now known as the golden rule, promotes sensitivity to the preferences of others.

Good measure, pressed down, shaken together and running over refers to the marketplace. Grain was poured out, shaken down, and then filled to overflowing to ensure buyers received the full amount of their purchases. Those who are generous will experience generosity while those who are stingy will experience scarcity.

Jesus' *Sermon on the Plains* concludes with a series of short sayings that illustrates the character those who follow Jesus should display.

INSIGHTS

Jesus departed for a time of prayer and solitude (6.12), then He returned to His disciples (6.13) and finally went out to teach and heal (6.17). Today, we tend to do these activities in reverse order. We start with ministry, spend time in the community, and devote whatever little is left (often nothing at all) to solitude. Jesus' order is important. By devoting ourselves first to prayer and solitude, we give the Holy Spirit an opportunity to teach, impart wisdom, give us direction, etc., *before* we get busy doing what we think God would have us do.

1. Jesus called His followers to love their enemies, do good to those who hated them, bless those who cursed them, and pray for those who abused them. If Jesus were standing in front of you today, how well would He say you are living out His instructions? What are two practical ways you can love, do good, bless, or pray for those who oppose or have opposed you?

2. Jesus suggested that all those who hear His words and do them are like a house with a solid foundation that is not affected by floods. Why did Jesus make this comparison? How can you build a solid foundation to your life? Why is it important to have the foundation in place before the storms of life come?

Luke 7

BACKGROUND

Because the footwear of Jesus' time was primarily sandals, foot washing was a part of the general hospitality of the times. The function was generally left to the servants.

A kiss was a common sign of affection and greeting, even between men.

OVERVIEW

The widow, having lost her husband, was already on the lower rungs of society. Without her son, she would have no one to care for her and little means of providing for herself. Jesus saw her, knew what she faced, and had compassion. Touching a dead body made Jesus ceremonially unclean (Num. 19.11), yet Jesus' compassionate touch was always in places that were dirty and undignified.

When Jesus forgave the sins of the woman who washed His feet, He said, "her sins, which are many, *are* forgiven" (7.47; emphasis added). The statement was made in the present tense and pointed to an action that had already taken place. Jesus did not require anything of the woman before making the pronouncement and responding to her faith in Him.

Jesus called John more than a prophet because he filled a special role by fulfilling Isaiah 40.3 and proclaiming the coming of the Messiah. For Jews, the Messiah was expected to lead them in a new exodus that would free them from the captivity of a foreign ruler. Rather than providing temporary freedom from the physical and political bondage thc people experienced, the Messiah whom John heralded provided everlasting freedom from spiritual bondage.

Children often engaged in games of make-believe that included imitating weddings and funerals. Jesus used this analogy to refer to His present generation, particularly the religious leaders, who were dissatisfied with both Jesus and John the Baptist even though the two men had very different approaches to their call to the people to take up the faith.

It was considered virtuous to have a visiting or well-known teacher as guest for a meal. Religious leaders often opened their homes to the poor of the community when having a banquet. These uninvited people were expected to sit quietly and observe the exchange between the invited guests.

Perfume by itself was not considered sinful. Because this woman was considered sinful, she was likely a prostitute who would have used perfume in her profession. Accepting such a gift would have been offensive to the religious leaders of the day.

Jesus' parable of the two debtors whose financial obligations were forgiven went far beyond the conventions of the day. Though debts were to be relieved every seventh year, creditors often found a way around this obligation to ensure their own finances were not threatened.

Luke made a point of showing that Jesus broke many of the social taboos of the times to reach out to those who endured discrimination and marginalization. In very quick succession, Jesus is shown reaching out to those alienated racially (7.1-10), economically (7.11-17), religiously (7.24-35), and morally (7.36-50).

INSIGHTS

Jesus did not directly answer John's question about whether He was the Messiah. Instead, He left it to John to come to his own conclusion based on the evidence presented to him. We must do the same today. God does not force Himself on any of us. Instead, He waits patiently for us to make our own decision. Just as with John, however, He always gives us enough evidence to make the right decision. It is usually our human pride, selfishness, and self-centeredness that prevent us from seeing that which God plainly presents.

1. Though John the Baptist understood his call to announce the coming Messiah and had witnessed the dove descend on Jesus when Jesus was baptized, he still had doubts. Instead of directly responding to those doubts, Jesus suggested John the Baptist look to those whom He had healed for an answer. What doubts have you struggled with? How do you find answers to those doubts? How can the experiences of other believers serve to bolster your own faith?

2. Simon's indignation was tempered by the parable of the two debtors. Though not all of us have dramatic conversion stories or have turned from lives of great sin in order to follow Jesus, we all have been given an unbelievable gift, the forgiveness of our sins. How much do you appreciate the gift of forgiveness and resulting relational restoration with God? Are there any times you have a tendency to take it for granted? How do you relate the tremendous value of this gift to those around you?

LUKE 8

BACKGROUND

Though called a sea, the Sea of Galilee is actually a large lake. The high hills and mountains surrounding the Sea of Galilee funnel the cooler air of the mountains down river ravines to the lake. When this cooler air meets the warm air of the lake, violent storms can arise out of nowhere. Even experienced fishermen feared being on the sea when this type of storm hit.

OVERVIEW

Parables were usually used to illustrate a point rather than to conceal it. Sometimes, however, Jewish and Greek teachers would tell the story without elaborating on the point the story made. Only those who listened carefully would discern its truth. Often, Jesus' parables contained truth and judgment. For those who understood the parable, new truth about God's kingdom was revealed. For those who did not understand or would not accept the truth, judgment was evident.

Agriculture was a common method of making a living. As a result, many of the people listening would be able to relate to the image of the parable.

The lamps Jesus referred to in the illustration of the light were small clay lamps that were set on lamp stands in order for their light to shine around a room. The parable served as an encouragement to proclaim God's truth, once known, instead of keeping it to one's self.

Jesus was not disparaging His family. Rather, He was expanding the definition of family to include all who obeyed God's word.

The control exhibited by Jesus to calm the storm was attributed to God in the Old Testament. Such display of a godly power by a human would have caused great awe and fear.

In ancient times, knowing the name of another was thought to give power over that person. The demons' attempt to wield this type of power over Jesus proved useless.

A legion consisted of four to six thousand troops; therefore, this man is thought to have been home to a large number of demons. The herd of swine that drowned in the lake would support this notion.

The woman's flow of blood made her unclean. Coming in contact with any other person would have made them ceremonially unclean for the remainder of the day. As a result, it took a great deal of courage for the woman to seek out Jesus.

The reason Jesus commanded Jairus and his family not to tell anyone about the revival of his daughter is unclear, especially since Jesus had just told the demon possessed man to stay in his community and tell everyone all He had done.

Luke recorded four miracles in this section of his writings. As a whole, they illustrate Jesus' command over diverse phenomena—nature, demons, disease, and death. Each one strikes closer to the person and shows the comprehensiveness of Jesus' authority.

INSIGHTS

The parable of the four types of soil is very applicable today. Some people hear God's Word but never fully understand it, and instead, follow the ways of the world. Some people have a superficial encounter with the Truth, but never spend time mediating and studying. When times get difficult, they abandon God's Word for the ways of the world. Some people hear and understand God's Word, but choose the riches and pleasures of the world over God's Truth. Finally, some people hear, understand, and apply what they have heard to live richly fulfilling and productive godly lives.

1. When the storm on the Sea of Galilee put the disciples in danger, they called upon Jesus, who immediately calmed the seas. How have you seen Jesus bring peace and calm to the storms of life? Do you wait until you are in danger, as the disciples did, or do you invite Jesus into the threatening circumstances early on? Though Jesus doesn't always take away the storms of our lives, He always walks with us through them. What can you do to rely more fully on Jesus' presence when trials and suffering are a part of your life?

2. When Jesus spoke of lighting the lamp and placing it where it could be seen, He was referring to our spiritual light. How well do you share God's truth with those around you, especially those who live in spiritual darkness? What keeps you from sharing with others when you have the opportunity? What is one practical thing you can do to increase your confidence in proclaiming the good news?

Luke 9

BACKGROUND

Herod the Great was the ruler of Judea when Jesus was born. After his death, his kingdom was divided among three of his sons, Archelaus, Herod Antipas (also known as Herod the Tetrarch), and Herod Philip II. Technically, the term tetrarch refers to the ruler of one-fourth of a country, although the title can also be used in place of *king* or *prince.* Herod Antipas ruled over Galilee and Perea (an area to the south of Galilee and west of the Jordan River), and Jesus would eventually appear before him.

OVERVIEW

By sending the twelve out, Jesus not only extended His power and authority to His disciples, He gave them practical experience. Jesus' specification that the twelve travel light meant they had to rely upon God's provision for their needs.

The feeding of the five thousand is the only miracle to appear in all four Gospels (Matt. 14.13-21; Mk. 6.30-44; Jn. 6.5-14).

Luke continues his theme of who Jesus is when he included Jesus' question, "Who do the crowds/you say that I am?" Though the disciples thought the crowd would answer by citing one of the Old Testament prophets, Peter believed Jesus was the Christ or Messiah. There were a number of views regarding what the Messiah would look like. Most had a political focus and expectation of deliverance from foreign rulers as well as the formation of an earthly kingdom.

The *cross* was the horizontal beam that the condemned carried out to the site of execution. Generally, the route was through crowds who jeered and taunted the condemned. Jesus' reference to the cross gave an indication of the scorn, derision, and rejection His followers would face as they proclaimed a true but unpopular message to the world.

Jesus' appearance on the mountainside in glorified form with Moses and Elijah is known as the transfiguration. The heavenly endorsement echoed the endorsement made when Jesus was baptized (3.22). This time, God urged the hearers to heed the words of His Son. Jesus' command that the disciples keep quiet about the events they had seen may have been because the men did not yet fully understand what had been revealed.

Jesus hinted at the disciples' lack of faith as the reason they were unable to cast the demon out of the boy. Jesus' power and authority were again evident as He used only a command to cast the demon out.

Status was of great importance to the Jewish people and the disciples' argument likely stemmed from this. Children had no status in Jewish society, so Jesus' analogy points to the differing norms in His kingdom.

Samaritans were the descendants of Jews who married Gentiles. Jews didn't recognize Samaritans as true inheritors of God's kingdom, so hostility existed between the two.

Proper burial of one's parents was a significant responsibility for a son. Jesus' urging to forsake this task was a radical departure from tradition and seemed to encourage disobedience to one of the commandments. In reality, Jesus was stating that nothing should be placed higher than devotion to Him.

INSIGHTS

In Jesus' day, just as today, many people spent their time and energy advancing and/or accumulating very temporary issues/goods. Jesus warned that those who lived in that manner would eventually lose not only what they had spent so much time and energy on, but their very lives as well. On the other hand, those who focused their time and energy on things with eternal value would not only realize a great reward but also enjoy eternal life themselves.

1. Jesus' question about who He is is the most important question we can answer. How do you answer this question? How would you respond to an unbeliever's curiosity about why Jesus is so important in the Christian faith?

2. The disciples wanted the man who was casting out demons in Jesus' name to stop. How does Jesus' reply apply today? How can we use His reply to help bring unity to our houses and communities in the midst of great denominational divide?

Luke 10

BACKGROUND

Sodom was used as the embodiment of sinfulness and refers to God's destruction of the city (Gen. 18.20-19.29). Numerous references in the Old Testament use Sodom as a symbol of the sin and judgment that will be realized by other cities, nations, and people who are not obedient to God and His ways (Deut. 32.32; Is. 13.19; Jer. 49.18; Amos 4.11).

OVERVIEW

Though Jesus' focus was on training the twelve disciples, He also ensured there were others ready to go out and continue the work He started. The seventy-two were sent out with instructions similar to those of the twelve and Jesus was upfront about the reaction they could expect as they moved about the country.

A lamb among wolves conveyed an image of defenselessness and was a common analogy in Jesus' time.

Those who refused to hear and accept the message Jesus sent His disciples out with were to be considered akin to the dust of pagan cities, which was wiped off to avoid causing defilement of the Holy Land.

Chorazin (also Korazin) and Bethsaida were both located on the shore of the Sea of Galilee. Tyre and Sidon were both Phoenician cities located north of Israel. Jesus' use of these cities was meant to jolt the people into realizing the significance of their rejection of His message. Hades is sometimes translated as *the depths* and is Greek for hell.

Exorcists of the day employed a variety of means to persuade demons to leave. The ability to use only Jesus' name amazed the disciples and gave them reason to rejoice. Jesus, however, reminded them that the greatest reason to rejoice resulted from their acceptance of Jesus and His message and their consequential position as God's children.

Jesus' prayer that things were hidden from the wise and prudent and revealed to babes (children) would have been offensive to the scribes who studied hard to understand the scriptures and God's law.

It was common in Jesus' time for people to test rabbis by posing difficult questions. Jesus' initial response to the lawyer was not an indication that good works would lead to eternal life. Rather, obedience to God and His commands is a natural result of receiving salvation solely through placing one's faith in Him.

Jesus didn't directly answer the question of who a neighbor is. Instead, He showed the listeners how to act as a neighbor by providing what is needed.

The Samaritan's compassion was expressed in both time and money. His two denarii would have typically paid for approximately 24 days of care[5] and he was willing to do more as was necessary.

Jesus' parable forced the questioner to answer his own question by choosing a person he would have hated.

Disciples often sat at the feet of their teachers. Seeing a woman in such a position would have shocked most men of Jesus' time. Hospitality was highly valued in the Jewish culture and women played a significant role in providing it. Yet, Jesus affirmed Mary's role, attesting to both the importance of assimilating Jesus' teaching and women's place in doing so.

INSIGHTS

Jesus sent his disciples out to spread His message of salvation. Those who heard the messengers heard the message and received salvation. It was not the messenger who was important but the message itself. The same is true today. We are called to spread the good news to those around us. Who they hear the message from is not as important as

[5] Earl Radmacher, Ronald B. Allen, and H. Wayne House, editors, *Nelson's New Illustrated Bible Commentary* (Nashville: Thomas Nelson Publishers), 1273

hearing the message. It is then up to each individual to accept or reject what they have heard. They cannot use the messenger as an excuse for rejecting the message.

1. Why did Jesus warn the disciples that He was sending them out as lambs among wolves? What does this say about what we should expect when we proclaim the good news of Christ? How does the fact that the harvest is plentiful but the laborers are few serve as an encouragement for proclaiming God's word?

2. The parable of the Good Samaritan dramatically redefined the word neighbor in Jesus' listeners' minds. How would you define neighbor? Can you relate to any of the characters in the parable? How often do you look for opportunities to be a good Samaritan to someone in need?

Luke 11

BACKGROUND

Jonah delivered God's message to Nineveh, whose inhabitants responded by repenting of their wrongdoing (Jon. 3.5-10). Solomon confirmed reports of God's wisdom and blessings on him during the Queen of Sheba's (queen of the South) visit and she responded by acknowledging the God of the Jews (1 Kgs. 10.1-9). Both the Ninevites and the queen were Gentiles or pagans who, on the surface, were unlikely respondents to God's message.

OVERVIEW

In response to how to pray, Jesus gave both a prayer that could be prayed and a model on which to base other prayers. *The Lord's Prayer* provides an example of the number and variety of requests that can be presented to God in prayer. The requests, however, are preceded by recognition of God's divinity and holiness, as well as a desire to see God's will and plan come to pass. The requests include:

- *Daily bread* – recognition of one's dependence on God for all daily needs
- *Forgive us our sins* – recognition of sin as a debt to God and the need for His merciful response
- *We forgive others* – recognition that the mercy sought from God must be extended to others
- *Lead us not into temptation* – recognition of the need for spiritual protection in order to avoid sin

Hospitality was considered an essential duty regardless of the time of day or night the request was made. When no food was available for a guest, one had the choice of being rude or seeking food from a neighbor. Jesus was illustrating to the disciples that they must be bold and persistent as they prayed to God.

Jesus' counsel to ask, seek, and knock was not a guarantee that whatever was asked for in prayer would be received. Rather, it was a reminder that God would respond with that which was spiritually beneficial (i.e. good gifts) when the petitioner prayed boldly in that vein.

Accusing Jesus of casting out demons by Beelzebub (a Philistine god) was akin to accusing Jesus of blasphemy. Jesus' response showed the lack of logic in the accusation. Casting out demons by the power of a demon would be to undo what Satan had done, thereby defeating Satan's own purposes.

The finger of God was a reference to His power and alluded to Pharaoh and his magicians in Exodus (8.19).

Praising a child by blessing his/her mother was a common practice of the times. Jesus was careful, however, to point to where true blessings come from: knowledge of and obedience to the Word of God.

Jesus used light as a metaphor for truth and falsehood. Focusing on truth would fill one with light or goodness while focusing on falsehood would fill one with darkness or evil.

The Pharisee with whom Jesus ate referred to ceremonial cleaning that is mentioned in the Old Testament, but not commanded (Gen. 18.4, Judg. 19.21). Pharisees were very concerned with outward appearances but paid little attention to their inner heart attitudes. Jesus used the visual image of the cup to illustrate this point. As Jesus continued, He included lawyers in His rebuke of the Pharisees. Traditions had developed around the Law of Moses that put a great strain on the people. Neither group did anything to relieve the strain. Instead, they pridefully pointed to their own apparent ability to adhere to the Law.

INSIGHTS

Jesus said, "He who is not with Me is against Me." Every person must make his/her own decision about whether Jesus is who He said He was. He leaves no room for neutrality. Either Jesus is the Son of God, or He is not. The viewpoint that Jesus was simply a good teacher is not logical. A good teacher would not continually claim to be someone he was not as Jesus claimed to be God. To continually assert a false claim would not make one a good teacher. Only two choices exist, either Jesus was crazy or He was the Son of God. Our eternal future rests on making the right choice.

1. It can be easy to recite memorized prayers, such as *The Lord's Prayer,* without much thought. When you used memorized prayers, how can you ensure they are not just a rote recitation but intentional and meaningful? How can you use *The Lord's Prayer* as a guide for your own personal prayers? Is there any part of this prayer—praising God, praying God's will to be done, making requests, asking for and giving forgiveness, protection against sin—that needs to be a more prominent part of your prayers?

2. Jesus accused the Pharisees of looking good to those around them but being filled with sin. Are there any sins, especially secret sins, you try to hide from others so you look good to them? Why is living an authentic, transparent life important to God? What steps can you take—confessing, repenting, committing to turning from a specific sin, being held accountable—to ensure what people see on the outside is who you are on the inside?

LUKE 12

BACKGROUND

The Ten Commandments ended with an injunction not to covet possessions belonging to a neighbor. Jesus extended that commandment to include coveting possessions in general. Just as acquiring a neighbor's possessions would serve no good purpose, so acquiring possessions for the sake of the possessions also has no value.

OVERVIEW

By picking a naturally acoustic setting, such as a hillside or cove, a speaker could address a large gathering of people.

Leaven (yeast used to make dough rise) was often used as a synonym for corruption. Only a small amount is needed in comparison to the amount of flour. It points to how a small amount of sin or corruption can have a large impact and devastating effect.

A variety of birds could be found in the marketplace, the cheapest of which were sparrows and were most often eaten by the poor. Jesus used a common Jewish argument form that often contained the words *how much more* and compared one known value or thing to another less known. Here, just as God knows every sparrow, so He knows each of His children, right down to the hairs on their heads.

Though Jesus was the Son of God, His deity was veiled while on earth, and therefore, denial of Jesus would be forgiven. The Holy Spirit, however, was the Spirit of Jesus and came to testify to the truth of Jesus. Denial or blasphemy against Holy Spirit was, then, a blatant rejection of the work of Jesus, which would not be forgiven.

Jesus spoke against the high value placed on possessions, first by responding to the request to judge the inheritance between two brothers, second through the parable of the rich man hoarding his grain, and finally through trusting in God's provision.

In the parable of the rich landowner, the words *I* or *my* appear ten times, pointing to the selfish focus that resulted from the man's good fortune. Jesus does not condemn the possessions, but rather the man's perspective that what he had was his alone to hoard.

Jesus challenged His listeners to trust God to provide for their needs rather than worry about where food and clothing would come from. Trusting God extended to not worrying about the future, which is rarely affected by any degree of worry. Possessions are often sought as an end in themselves, but all eventually disintegrate and have no lasting value. Jesus encouraged His listeners to focus instead on that which had lasting value: relationships with God and other people. Using possessions to accomplish God's purpose results in eternal rewards that will not disintegrate.

Girding one's waist meant pulling up the hem of a robe to enable a man to run.

Jesus likened the disciples to servants who had to be constantly ready for their masters' return, which could take place at any hour of the day or night. Several types of servants were described, but the wise servant is the one who dealt righteously with all that belonged to the master, even during his absence. The absent master was an allusion to the time between Jesus' first appearance on earth and His second coming.

Fire was an image of God's judgment. Though Jesus was ready for the judgment of humankind to take place, other events had to first unfold.

INSIGHTS

Just as it was easy for the people of Jesus' day to get caught up in what they owned, so it is for us today. The world constantly tells us our value lies in what we possess. The adage "he who dies with the most toys wins" places our focus directly on continually acquiring more and better things. But Jesus taught that things, especially the accumulation of things, have no lasting value. The true value of possessions comes only from their use to achieve God's purposes. As such, it is only in giving them away or using them to serve other people that they truly gain any value.

1. In the parable of the rich farmer, the farmer horded for himself what could have benefited others. Are any of your attitudes toward your possessions displeasing to God? Are there any possessions you have in abundance that would be of greater value to others if you gave them away? If God were to call you home tomorrow, would you have any regrets? What changes can you make to ensure you have no regrets whenever it is God calls you home?

2. Jesus warned against fearing those who can kill the body (temporal) without fearing Him who has the power to cast the soul to hell (eternal). Does God inhabit the proper place in your life? Do you have an eternal perspective in your day-to-day activities? In what areas of your life might you fear people and what they think more than you fear God?

Luke 13

BACKGROUND

The tower of Siloam was likely located in the southern wall of Jerusalem. The collapse of the wall is not attested to anywhere else in scripture and is thought to be the result of natural events rather than a human induced incident. Earthquakes were common in the area and provide one possibility.

OVERVIEW

Many cultures of the time believed that a person's unexpected or premature death was punishment for extreme sin. Since all people die, Jesus' reference to perishing was an eternal death, which would come to anyone who did not repent of his/her sins.

In the parable of the fig tree, the man represented God while the tree represented Israel. Just as a fruit tree's purpose was to bear fruit and it had no value if it did not, so Israel also was to *bear fruit* or suffer judgment. Israel's fruit came through repentance of sins and serving as a witness to the nations.

Loosened was often used to describe physical healing or being freed from demon possession.

The synagogue ruler was quick to point out Jesus' transgression of the law prohibiting work on the Sabbath. Jesus verbally outmaneuvered the synagogue ruler by pointing out the basic compassion shown to animals could rightfully be extended to people.

Daughter of Abraham was a term of endearment that showed how much the woman was valued by God.

Both the mustard seed and leaven were small in comparison to what they produced, i.e. a mustard tree 8-12 feet tall and a loaf of bread. Though Jesus and His disciples were small in number, especially when compared to the Jewish establishment and the Roman government, God's kingdom could and would be established through them.

The parable about entering through the narrow gate referred to experiencing salvation on God's terms. Those who accepted Jesus (the narrow gate) would enter into eternal life. Those who attempted to achieve salvation on their own terms would be rejected when they knocked on the door for access. Associating with Jesus (eating and drinking in His presence, listening to His teaching in the streets) was not enough. Only those whom Jesus personally knew would be permitted to enter.

Most Jews believed that salvation and God's coming kingdom was reserved for the Jewish people. While many people of the time might have interpreted Jesus' reference to the east, west, north, and south as a gathering of the Jewish people from the places to which they had been scattered, in the context of Luke and Acts, Jesus was referring to all people everywhere.

The Pharisees' warning that Herod (Antipas) wanted to kill Jesus may have been an excuse to get Him to move out of their vicinity. Herod had killed John the Baptist and others so the threat could have just as easily been legitimate.

In Jesus' day, referring to someone as a *fox* was akin to calling him worthless or cunning in an unprincipled manner.

The reference to being perfected on the third day was an allusion to Jesus' coming resurrection.

Jesus quoted Psalm 118.26, the refrain the people would proclaim when Jesus finally entered Jerusalem.

INSIGHTS

People want to define their own terms for gaining entrance into heaven. For some, this path includes perfecting the inner self and tapping into the power of a "higher being". For others, focus is on being a good person. Still others believe that Buddha, Muhammad, or a plethora of other false gods provide the key to salvation. Defining one's own path may seem beneficial in the short term, but it has long-term negative consequences. Jesus made it very clear in all His teachings that there is only one way to enjoy eternal life and that is through believing in Him alone.

1. Jesus used a term of endearment when He called the bent over woman a daughter of Abraham. Do you know how much God values you? How do you respond when someone tells you that God delights in you and passionately loves you? If you are uncomfortable with how worthy you are in God's eyes, what can you do to begin to see yourself through God's eyes?

2. The parable about entering through the narrow gate is just as applicable today as in Jesus' time. In what ways do you see the world trying to enter heaven through a gate other than the narrow gate? Why do you think Jesus is so adamant about there being only one gate through which people can enter? Are you certain you are on the path that leads to the narrow gate? If you are not, what can you do to gain that assurance?

Luke 14

BACKGROUND

Proverbs 25.6-7 states one should not exalt oneself in the presence of a king or stand in the place of great men because it is better to be brought up than put down. Jesus expanded this proverb when He told the parable about the seating order at a banquet.

OVERVIEW

It was common practice in Jesus' time for a prominent teacher to be invited as an honored guest to a meal with a Jewish family.

Dropsy (called edema today) occurs when fluid builds up in the body causing swelling. It is the symptom of a variety of medical conditions.

In Jewish debates, silence or the inability to respond to an argument would indicate either the silent party had lost the debate or they were ignorant of the law and, therefore, unable to respond.

Seating arrangements indicating social status were very important at both Jewish and Roman banquets.

In response to the man's excitement about eating at the banquet table of God, Jesus issued a warning through a parable. Invitations to banquets were generally sent out well in advance and those who responded would have received a second notice that the banquet was ready. Each excuse was weak. Land would have been inspected before it was bought. The same was true for oxen and the fact that this man owned five indicates enough wealth that a servant could have freed the master to fill his obligation. Men were exempt from military service for the first year of marriage (Deut. 24.5), but this did not excuse them from social obligations. The master's second invitation invited those not normally present at such banquets: poor, crippled (or maimed), blind, and lame. The final invitation extended out into the countryside and the people least likely to be present at a wealthy man's banquet.

Through the parable, Jesus gave a picture of who might be present at God's banquet table. Those one might well expect to be present would be absent because of their refusal to respond to Jesus' message. Instead, those least likely to be guests in the eyes of the world were more likely to be in attendance. The invitation to those in the countryside may have pointed to the inclusion of Gentiles.

Jesus' statement that anyone who followed Him had to hate his family was hyperbole (an exaggerated statement used to make a point but not to be taken literally). Fearing family rejection, disapproval, or even persecution was not a legitimate excuse for not following Jesus.

Jesus was not asking for an emotional response to His call, a response that would be quickly forgotten when the going got tough. Instead, He wanted His disciples to count the cost; to know what would be required going into the commitment they were making. This was no different from a builder or a king who knows prior to committing to his endeavor what is needed to complete the task.

INSIGHTS

Hospitality and service, even today, are often given with ulterior motives such as payment for an invitation, an attempt to relieve guilt, in hopes of obligating the receiver to give in return, or to maintain a certain social status or obligation. Jesus taught, however, that acts should be performed with purer motives. When hospitality and services are extended with no expectation of repayment, especially to those with no means of repaying, they are given with the right motives.

1. Luke recorded multiple episodes of Jesus healing on the Sabbath. The Pharisees were angered by Jesus' apparent disregard for the laws against work on the Sabbath and unable to answer the question of whether what He did was, in fact, lawful or not. What is the purpose of observing a Sabbath, or day of rest, once a week? In what ways can following a list of rules about what can and can't be done on such a day take the focus away from the true intention of observing the Sabbath? What is the risk of having no boundaries at all in relation to the Sabbath?

2. Jesus' imperative that His followers must hate their mothers and fathers, wives and children, brothers and sisters, and even their own lives seems extreme. Was Jesus saying that family was not important? What was Jesus getting at in making this statement? How do you go about making this directive a part of your efforts to follow Jesus?

Luke 15

BACKGROUND

Pharisees followed strict guidelines of behavior. Their focus was on maintaining a standard of righteousness among those in their community. Often their self-righteousness was justified by comparing themselves to those around them. They avoided contact with known sinners, especially at meal times, as intimate fellowship during a meal implied acceptance. Jesus continually took exception to the Pharisees' behavior and strove to open their eyes to what it meant to truly be godly.

OVERVIEW

Jesus told three parables, all of which focus on rejoicing with friends over finding what had been lost and directed toward the self-righteous Pharisees. Through these parables, Jesus was implying that anyone who did not rejoice when a sinner repented was not a friend of God's.

The value of what was found increased with each parable: first one of one hundred, then one of ten, and finally one of two.

It was not uncommon for other Jewish teachers to emphasize God's forgiveness of those who repented, but few spoke of God seeking out sinners.

A flock of one hundred sheep was average sized and would likely have had two or three shepherds watching over it. The head shepherd would have been free to search for the missing sheep, knowing that the balance of the flock was being well cared for.

The stone floors of the poor had many crevices and cracks into which small items could easily fall. This happened often enough that archaeologists now use the coins found in these crevices to date when people lived in the houses.

In the parable of the coins, the comparison to sinners is again made, with the angels rejoicing this time.

The parable of the lost son spoke closest to the attitude of the Pharisees. In the parable, the lost son represents sinners, the father represents God, and the elder son represents the Pharisees. Jesus' point in the parable was that while God was rejoicing over the return of a sinner, despite the sinner having been almost inconceivably rebellious and inconsiderate, the Pharisees saw only reason to grumble and complain.

In Jewish culture, for a son to ask for his inheritance before the father died would have been akin to saying the father was already dead. A Jewish father in this situation would have been within his bounds to severely punish the son. The father granting the son's request would have been difficult for Jesus' hearers to understand or appreciate.

The eldest son received a double portion of the inheritance upon his father's death (Deut. 21.17). In this case, the elder son would have received two-thirds and the younger son one-third of the total estate.

Pigs were considered unclean according to the Law of Moses (Deut. 14.8). Therefore, feeding pigs would have been one of the most humiliating jobs a Jewish person could do.

The father showed great compassion to his son by running to meet him. Any dignified Jewish man would not run.

I have sinned was a confession of sin. Once made, the younger son relied completely on the mercy of his father.

The older son focused on justice, which had not been done in his eyes. His final response to the father's plea to join in the celebration is not recorded, inviting the listener to reflect on the proper response to the situation.

INSIGHTS

Volumes of books have been written and many sermons delivered on the parable of the Prodigal Son. Though most focus on the younger son (the return of a sinner), it is also worth looking at the parable from the perspective of the father (God's rejoicing over saved sinners) and the elder brother (stubborn and self-righteous, he refused to acknowledge the joy of another's good fortune).

1. Most Christians can relate to having acted like both sons in the parable of the Prodigal Son at different times of their lives. What aspect of the parable can you most relate to and why? How does the parable encourage you to change your attitude or actions? How confident are you that your heavenly Father is as eagerly awaiting you when you have sinned as the father in the parable? Since God *always* awaits us with eager anticipation, how can you have greater confidence in this truth?

2. In each of the parables in this chapter, there is great rejoicing when the lost item or person is found. How quickly do you rejoice when an unbeliever places his/her faith in Jesus? Do you pray your worst enemies have a life-changing encounter with Jesus? Is there anyone you secretly believe is underserving of receiving everlasting life if s/he places her/his faith in Jesus? How would your argument hold up if you were able to make it directly to God?

LUKE 16

BACKGROUND

In Jewish and other ancient Near East cultures, divorce was permitted for almost any reason. Jesus' teaching on the subject was much stricter than anyone else's at the time. Luke recorded Jesus' statement on divorce in absolute terms, though Matthew recorded a similar statement that included an exception (Matt. 5.32, 19.9). Paul also spoke on the issue and included an exception (1 Cor. 7.12-15). Although divorce was permitted under certain exceptions, it is never presented as the preferred option.

OVERVIEW

The master's debtors would have likely rented land from the master and owed him their rental fee from their harvest. Though the amount owed by each debtor was different, the value would have been approximately the same. In times of hardship, landowners would often reduce what was owed to them in return for a benevolent public image. Had the master gone back to the debtors and demanded full payment, his benevolent image would have been damaged.

The master's compliment and lack of further action against the steward suggest the steward may not have done anything illegal. The steward may have been shrewd within the law by:

- Lowering the price by his rightful authority;
- Adhering to the law by removing the interest charge from the debt (Lev. 25.36-37);
- Removing his own commission.

Even if the steward had acted illegally, Jesus was not commending the steward's behavior. Jesus' point in the parable was that all people have only what God has given them, so as stewards of His goods, they should be used wisely to make a lasting impact.

Jesus followed the parable with comments centered on the idea that small actions now, whether right or wrong, will manifest themselves in larger similar actions later.

Some translations use the term mammon to describe what people may be tempted to serve. It is an Aramaic term meaning money and possessions.

Jesus' point about heaven and earth passing away before the law failed was that it would be more likely for heaven and earth to end than for any of God's Word to be inaccurate.

The parable about the rich man and Lazarus was a warning to heed the law and live a life of generosity. Those who chose to ignore the law would not be persuaded, even by something as miraculous as a resurrection.

INSIGHTS

Though Jesus' parable warned that resurrection would not be enough to persuade some people to believe the truth of Scripture's claims, Jesus' own resurrection caused many people to come to faith. The warning is still valid. Today, many people refuse to believe Christianity's truth because they prefer to live as they choose, rather than living the sacrificial and often persecuted life Jesus calls us to. Such choices may appear profitable in the short term but, just as in the parable, no one escapes God's final judgment.

1. In the parable of the unjust servant, the master commends his servant for acting shrewdly. What does it look like for Christians to act shrewdly? In what ways have you or do you act shrewdly? Are there any ways in which you can or should be acting more wisely with the items and talents God has given you to steward?

2. Jesus stated it is not possible to serve two masters. Are there any ways in which you attempt to serve God and money at the same time? Have you experienced having to choose between the two? What were the motivations for the choice you made? Can you see how serving money results in enslavement and bondage? In what ways can you or have you put money into a proper perspective?

Luke 17

BACKGROUND

Leprosy was a general term used to describe a variety of skin infections and diseases, which may or may not have been contagious. It would have included, but was not limited to, the common-day definition of leprosy. According to the Law of Moses, priests were responsible for determining the status of such infections and diseases and when an affected person could or could not reenter the community (Lev. 13.1-14.32).

OVERVIEW

Jesus recognized that temptation was always a part of a person's life, but strongly warned those who caused temptation in the life of another.

Stumble was often used metaphorically and meant to sin or fall away from faith.

Millstones were used for grinding wheat into flour. They came in two sizes, a smaller one often used by a woman or a larger, heavier one turned by a donkey. Jesus would have referred to the larger millstone, indicating there was no escape from punishment for those who intentionally caused another to sin.

Jesus called his followers to forgive others. Just as they were to use money generously, they were also to extend compassion generously.

Mustard seeds are one of the smallest known seeds, yet grow to produce a substantial plant. Mulberry trees have vast root systems that allow them to live up to six hundred years.

Landowners wealthy enough to own slaves generally had only a few who did double duty in the fields and the house. Jesus' point appears to be that faith, no matter how small, is something that grows as it is used.

Although Jesus healed ten lepers and all had equal reason to be thankful, only the foreigner who was despised by most Jews returned to give thanks. Physical healing was only part of what took place. Spiritual healing also took place as the man began a relationship with Christ.

When the kingdom of God would come and what it would look like were debated topics of the day. Some thought the time was unknown while others contended it would come when all of Israel repented. Jesus shifted the focus by implying that something of God's reign was already present.

Both Noah's generation and Sodom were used as images of evil. In both cases, people hardly paid attention to God and suffered judgment as a result.

Lot's wife ignored God's instructions and looked back to see the destroyed city. The action cost her her life (Gen. 19.14-17, 26).

In Greek, masculine pronouns were used whenever at least one member of the group was male. Therefore, what some translations designate as two men in bed was more likely a husband and wife.

Though the disciples asked where the judgment would take place, Jesus did not directly answer the question. Instead, He pointed to the birds (vultures in some translations, eagles in others) that would hover around the impending death that will accompany the judgment. Jesus is not only the source of salvation but also of judgment. Those who trust in Him will be safe, but those who reject Him will suffer eternal consequences.

INSIGHTS

Jesus gave the lepers no more instruction than to present themselves to the priests. In order to experience healing, they had to act in faith. Today, God often asks us to do the same. We may feel more comfortable seeing the evidence of our answered prayer first, but the answer most often comes as we exercise our faith, do as God directs and *then* experience the result.

1. Jesus willingly healed the ten lepers but was disappointed when only one returned to say thank you. How often do you express gratitude to God for the daily blessings you receive? When is it hardest for you to express gratitude? Is there any change in attitude God is asking you to make that would make gratitude easier to express? Do you readily express your gratitude to those around you? If not, what keeps you from doing so?

2. Jesus commanded His followers to repeatedly forgive those who ask for forgiveness. How easy do you find it to forgive repeat offenses? Is there anyone you are withholding forgiveness from? What keeps you from extending forgiveness? Have you experienced holding unforgiveness in your heart doing more harm to you than the person you haven't forgiven? Can you release any unforgiveness you are holding onto to God and trust that He will bring both justice and mercy to the circumstances?

Luke 18

BACKGROUND

Some have thought that the *eye of the needle* was a small or narrow gate into Jerusalem designed to permit limited access to the city after the main gates had been closed for the night. The size of the gate required camels to be unloaded of the baggage or riders in order to squeeze through. However, no evidence, either Biblical or otherwise, has been found to support this explanation. Instead, the statement should be taken as hyperbole, an exaggerated statement used to make a point.

OVERVIEW

Luke included a remark at the beginning of the parable to explain why Jesus told it.

Widows were the ultimate example of the oppressed since they did not have anyone to support them. The judge, perhaps a secular judge because he did not fear God, was insensitive to the needs of the helpless. The important point of the parable is the widow's persistence, which Jesus used as an example of how His followers should pray. Jesus was not indicating that God withholds answers to prayers. Rather, He was showing that if an insensitive judge responded to a persistent widow, God would respond even more to the prayers of believers.

The Pharisee was portrayed as self-righteous and arrogant. He used *I* five times in two sentences, looked down on those around him, and was proud of his fasting and tithing. The tax collector, on the other hand, was humble as he approached God in repentance. *Went to his house justified* means declared righteous and forgiven.

Children had no social status in the Jewish culture, and the disciples did not want their teacher's valuable time taken up by those viewed as undeserving of His time. Jesus, however, made it clear that not only were the children worthy of His time but that many *nobodies* would be found in God's kingdom.

Many in Jesus' time viewed wealth as a blessing God gave to those who were righteous; so the statement that a camel could go through the eye of a needle more easily than the rich could enter the kingdom of heaven would have been shocking and lead to the disciples' question, "Who then can be saved?" Jesus' response gives an explanation of the statement. Wealthy people tend to rely upon themselves because they have the resources needed that make reliance on others unnecessary. But no one can enter the kingdom of heaven strictly by relying on his or her own efforts. Instead, all must rely upon God, who is able to make the impossible possible.

Begging was the only option available to those who were blind, lame, or otherwise incapacitated and unable earn a living through conventional work. The blind man's exclamation of *Son of David* indicates he recognized Jesus as the Messiah. Jesus responded by recognizing his faith and healing him.

INSIGHTS

The blind man was able to "see" what many of the sighted people following Jesus were unable to see—Jesus was the promised Messiah. Today, it is just as easy for those free from affliction to miss what those suffering hardship see more clearly. As a result, it is dangerous to maintain an attitude of superiority in relation to those who appear to be less fortunate that we are. Our pride and self-righteousness can be more restricting and limiting than the physical, emotional, or mental afflictions from which some people suffer.

1. In what areas of your life do you need to apply the widow's persistence? When circumstances or people appear to be hopeless, how can persistence in prayer create room for hope? Do you have confidence that God answers prayer? If not, what are some ways you can seek to increase your confidence?

2. The rich ruler went away sad because he had many possessions. What place do possessions have in your life? Are you able to easily let go of them? Would your relationship with God benefit if you had fewer possessions? Why or why not? Is God calling you to sell some of your possession so that His kingdom work might be advanced?

Luke 19

BACKGROUND

A portion of Jesus' parable of the ten minas paralleled historical events. Though Jesus was not retelling history, the plot of the parable would have been familiar. Archelaus, son of Herod the Great, had to travel to Rome in order receive the right to rule Judea. Those opposing him made an appearance before Augustus Caesar. They were unsuccessful in persuading Augustus to appoint someone else to rule the region.

OVERVIEW

As *chief* tax collector, Zacchaeus would have been responsible for collecting a number of different taxes and would have had other tax collectors working under him. It is possible that he could have been wealthy without breaking any laws, but his offered restitution indicates he was conscious of participating in some unscrupulous activities.

Zacchaeus' restitution went beyond what the law prescribed. Fourfold or fivefold was required only for stealing sheep or oxen (Ex. 22.1). He offered his restitution in response to grace, not in order to receive it.

Most Jewish people believed they would experience salvation just because they were descendants of Abraham. Ongoing criminal activity (such as tax collecting) would remove one from receiving salvation. Jesus, however, extended salvation to Zacchaeus.

In response to the thoughts that God's kingdom would appear immediately, Jesus told a parable that showed otherwise. The nobleman represents Jesus who would depart the earth to return at an undetermined later date in order to assume His reign. In the meantime, He gives His subjects (followers) gifts that are to be used for the benefit of His kingdom. Those who have a good return to show for what they were given will be well rewarded while those who hoard their gifts will experience judgment.

A mina was equivalent to between three and four months' wages.

Bethphage and Bethany were about two miles east of Jerusalem while the Mount of Olives was located just outside of Jerusalem and directly across from the temple.

Political and religious leaders would often commandeer animals or other property for short-term use. As a result, this incident would not have been as strange as it might appear today.

The disciples found the donkey just where Jesus said it would be. Repeatedly in the last week of Jesus' life, events unfolded as He said they would. Jesus was in control of what happened to Him and nothing caught Him by surprise.

Spreading out clothing on the road was akin to our practice of rolling out the red carpet; it showed honor to the recipient.

The people's refrain as Jesus entered Jerusalem echoed Psalm 118.26 and added *king* in place of an unspecified *he.*

Approximately 40 years after Jesus wept over Jerusalem and predicted its demise, the Romans destroyed the city in response to a Jewish revolt.

Since the sellers made sacrifices available to those who visited from outside of Jerusalem, it seems unlikely that Jesus' action was directed at the practice of offering sacrifices, but rather at the way in which the sellers were conducting their business.

INSIGHTS

It is interesting to note that in addition to being commended by the master for producing a return on what he had given them, the two servants were rewarded for their job well done. Today we might expect that reward to be a nice vacation, bonus, car, or other luxury item.

Instead, each of the servants was rewarded with more work—authority over a number of cities. God created humans to work (before Adam sinned, he was given the task of tending and keeping the garden, Gen. 2.15) and it is always in doing God's work that we will find our greatest fulfillment. As much as we may try to avoid work, it is through work that God desires to bless us.

1. When Jesus told Zacchaeus He had come to seek and save the lost, He gave a summary statement of His purpose for coming to earth. How well are you able to articulate why it was necessary for Jesus to come to earth? How confident are you about sharing your faith with the Zacchaeuses of the world who are curious about Jesus? Do you appreciate that although you may not lead a person to faith when answering a question about Jesus, you may be an important stepping-stone to that person ultimately making the decision to follow Jesus?

2. In the eyes of the people, a tax collector like Zacchaeus was not someone who would one day enjoy eternal life, yet Jesus saw him through different eyes. Are there people whom you have judged as unworthy for God's kingdom? Would Jesus make the same judgment? Do you give people around you every opportunity to place their trust in Jesus? How often do you pray that your enemies will come to know the grace and mercy of God?

Luke 20

BACKGROUND

Sadducees were one of three major divisions of Judaism. The other two were Pharisees and Essenes. The Sadducees did not believe in the resurrection of the dead and, therefore, rejected the idea of any reward or retribution delivered after death. They also did not believe in the oral tradition the Pharisees held in high esteem and believed the Pentateuch (the first five books of the Bible) was the only source of spiritual authority.

OVERVIEW

Jesus' question concerning John's ministry posed a dilemma for the temple leaders. In addition to the stated reason, recognizing John's ministry as being from heaven would have allowed for the possibility that Jesus' was as well. Instead of taking a stand, the temple leaders avoided the issue by pleading ignorance.

Absentee landowners commonly allowed tenant farmers to work their land. Payment was generally made from the harvested crop and was either a percentage of the harvest or a set amount fixed at the time of the agreement.

The people responded in surprise to the parable of the vineyard because they understood the implication. The owner (God) would give His land (Israel's inheritance) to others (Gentiles) because of the poor treatment the tenant farmer's (religious leaders) showed the owner's servants (prophets) and son (Jesus). The idea that Israel's inheritance would be given to the Gentiles would have been grim for the Jewish people.

Some translations use capstone instead of cornerstone. Both were important in the construction of a building. The cornerstone was used to join the foundation of two walls of a building while the capstone was placed over a doorway, giving it stability.

The religious leaders' authority was limited to the functioning of the temple. Therefore, in order to rid themselves of Jesus, they tried to trap him into looking like a political revolutionary. Jesus, in seeing through their scheming, cleverly answered the question by indicating that taxes should be paid *and* God should be honored.

A woman left childless by the death of her husband was to be taken as a wife by a surviving brother who would father a child with the widow (Deut. 25.5). This law of levirate marriage perpetuated the name of the deceased brother.

Jesus dismissed the Sadducees attempt to highlight the absurdity of resurrection by affirming life in an *age to come*. Marriage would not be a part of that age, so the question did not apply. Jesus also noted that God would not have referred to Himself as the God of Abraham, Isaac, and Jacob if they no longer existed (Ex. 3.6).

Scribes, experts in the study of the Law of Moses, were pleased that Jesus' answer affirmed the resurrection but were intimidated, just as others had been, from asking further questions.

Jesus posed a theological issue to his listeners. The Messiah was to be the *Son of David*, yet David referred to the Messiah as Lord. He did not answer the question but pointed to the title *Lord* being more important than *Son of David*.

INSIGHTS

The Sadducees tried to validate their point of view by posing an absurd question about resurrection. We can be tempted to do the same today. Often we develop viewpoints based on our own rationale and don't make the effort to search the scriptures for what God says on the topic. At other times, we may not like what we understand God to say and devise an outcome that is more palatable. Ultimately, God's designs will be met, whether we agree or not, or like them or not. Both God's purposes and our own are better served by basing our views on what God says to be true.

1. Jesus used stories of things and events that were familiar to His listeners to relate harder to understand concepts to people. Have you ever thought about how important stories are in our lives? Have you thought about how you might use stories to help explain why you believe what you believe? What is one story from your own experience you might tell in order to help another person understand an aspect of God?

2. The chief priests, scribes, and elders immediately disliked the parable of the absentee landowner because of the implications it made about them. Is there anything God may be trying to tell you that you are not listening to because you don't like what He is saying? Is there any truth about yourself or those around you that you have been attempting to deny but would be better off acknowledging? Even in the midst of dealing with uncomfortable truths, are you able to trust that God loves you deeply and has your best interests in mind?

LUKE 21

BACKGROUND

Though one foundation wall still stands today, the temple was virtually destroyed approximately forty years after Jesus predicted it and Jerusalem was left in ruins in a war that lasted from 66-70 A.D. Jerusalem was completely destroyed a second time in 135 A.D., after which it was rebuilt as a pagan city with a pagan temple on the site of God's temple. Today, the Dome of the Rock has been built where the temple once stood. Muslims believe this is the place where Abraham sacrificed Isaac and Muhammad ascended to heaven.

OVERVIEW

A mite was a copper coin and was the smallest currency in use.

Jesus contrasted the rich who gave out of their excess to the giving of the widow who gave from what she needed to live on. Jesus' comparison indicated that God is more interested in the attitude with which giving is done than in the actual dollar amount given.

The temple was a splendid structure and served as the center of Jewish worship. Most Jews would have been appalled at the idea that the temple would one day be destroyed.

Though many would experience persecution as a result of their faith in Christ, no one would be separated from God. While some would die as a result of persecution, all would enjoy eternal life with God. In spite of and because of such persecution, God would give His people reason to testify to His presence and glory.

Jesus advised His listeners not to worry (meditate, in some

translations) about their defense beforehand. While this did not mean to go unprepared, it did mean to trust in God's provision and what would later be the Holy Spirit's input at the time it was needed.

As Jesus continued His discourse, He spoke of both the destruction of the temple and the end of the world. The two events are intertwined, with some believing the destruction of Jerusalem foreshadowed the end of the world.

The *time of the Gentiles* refers to a period when non-Jews would dominate and carry out God's plan. The fulfillment of the time of the Gentiles seems to indicate that Israel would once again be called upon to be God's agents.

Jesus' warning of the destruction of Jerusalem and the temple was similar to that of the Old Testament prophets who predicted God's divine judgment would come as a result of Israel's abandonment of the Mosaic covenant (the covenant made with Moses; Ex. 34.10-28).

Jesus' focus shifted to His second coming, which would include His authoritative return under the power and glory of God. Just as a budding tree signals the coming of spring, so Jesus' return will be signaled by signs that the end times are approaching.

For many, the signs of the end of time will bring great terror and fear. Those who have trusted in Christ, however, need not fear. For them, these signs are simply an indication that redemption is near.

The word *generation* (v. 32) can also mean *race* and may mean that the Jews will survive as a people until the end.

INSIGHTS

There have always been those who are bent on deceiving others. Either knowingly or because they themselves are deceived, the "truth" they share is really falsehood in God's eyes. Jesus warned that as the end times approach, those who teach lies as truth will become more numerous and more convincing. The best way we have to guard against becoming victims of such lies is to immerse ourselves in God's Word, to study His truth, the only truth, regularly. Then we will be better able to recognize and refute that which is not true.

1. Jesus commended the widow who offered all she had. How generous are you? Do you trust God completely to supply all your needs? Are you able to give sacrificially, as the widow did, or do you give only out of your abundance as the rich did? What, if any, adjustments in your attitude toward being generous might God want you to make?

2. Jesus warned His listeners to be aware of being deceived by the many that would come in His name. How do you guard against being deceived? How do you assess what you hear as being true or a lie? What steps might you take to increase your sensitivity to the validity or lack of validity of claims made by those around you?

Luke 22

BACKGROUND

Passover was the feast that commemorated Israel's deliverance from slavery in Egypt. A lamb was slaughtered and its blood put on the doorframe as a signal that God's angel should *pass over* the household. Any household not protected by the blood of a lamb experienced the death of all their firstborn males, animal as well as human (Ex. 12.1-13.16). The Feast of Unleavened Bread commemorated the Israelites' hasty departure from Egypt (Lev. 23.5-6).

OVERVIEW

Passion is the term often used to refer to Jesus' death and resurrection. Luke's accounting of these events begins with this chapter.

Passover and the Feast of Unleavened Bread were two different feasts with one immediately following the other. Because many pilgrims traveled to Jerusalem to celebrate both, they were often treated as a single celebration.

Women typically carried water jars, so a man carrying a water jar would have been easy to spot.

Judas's offer to betray Jesus simplified matters for the high priests, who could later claim that one of Jesus' own disciples precipitated His arrest.

Preparations for the Passover feast included purchasing a lamb, having it slaughtered at the temple, roasting the lamb whole, purchasing the other food items required for the Passover meal, preparing the food, and readying the room in which the meal would be enjoyed.

The Passover meal consisted of four courses and four cups. Luke mentioned one course (bread) and two cups (the first when Jesus stated He would not drink again until the kingdom of God came and the second He referred to as His blood). Luke, like the other gospel writers, included only that which was relevant to Jesus as the long anticipated Messiah.

With Jesus' words, the annual Passover meal celebrating Israel's freedom from Egyptian bondage became a more frequently shared meal celebrating humanity's freedom from the bondage of sin. Though it was not yet clear to the disciples, that freedom would come through Jesus' death and resurrection.

Blood was used to seal covenants, and Jesus' death and resurrection would initiate the New Covenant, which was open to anyone who responded to Jesus' offer of salvation.

While the Jews generally thought the Messiah would rule as an earthly king with all the power and authority accompanying such a position, Jesus showed that the Messiah was actually a servant leader who required those who followed after Him to lead in like manner.

Jesus knew what was to come would not only be difficult for Him but provide temptations for His disciples. He encouraged them to pray for strength.

In addition to a kiss being a sign of affection among family and friends, it was also a means for a disciple to show honor and submission to his teacher. As a result, Judas' kiss was an act of hypocrisy.

The council, or Sanhedrin, was a religious court consisting of seventy-one members representing three groups: leading priests, elders, and scribes. They met in a temple hall called the Chamber of Hewn Stone.

Claiming to be on par with God, as Jesus did when He would sit on the right hand of God, was considered blasphemous. Since all the council members heard Jesus' words, they could themselves serve as witnesses and had no need of calling others.

INSIGHTS

In the span of four to six hours, Peter went from wanting to protect Jesus by fighting (Peter struck the servant, John 18.10), to denying any knowledge of who Jesus was. We can experience the same vacillating commitment as we one moment vehemently defend what we know is right while in the next moment fail to come to the defense of someone in need. The good news is that just as Jesus forgave Peter and later called him to play an important role in the formation of the new church, God will also forgive our sincere repentance and continue to use us in causing His plans to come to pass.

1. In anticipation of His coming trial and crucifixion, Jesus withdrew with his disciples to pray. Though He encouraged them to pray, He found them asleep instead. What is your prayer life like? How would you rank your level of belief that God answers prayers? Are you fervent in prayer? Do you regularly and diligently pray for others when they share their requests with you? How might you make prayer a more meaningful and significant part of your life?

2. Peter boasted that he was willing to stay with Jesus regardless of what was to come, but instead, ended up denying he even knew Jesus. What areas of your life, if any, make you fearful to acknowledge your relationship with Jesus? Why can being forthright about who Jesus is in your life be so difficult? Have you ever taken the risk to acknowledge Jesus and seen God act in a spectacular way as a result? If so, what was the result?

Luke 23

BACKGROUND

Crucifixion was one of the most painful methods of torture and execution. The victim's wrists were tied and/or nailed to a crossbeam that was then hung on a vertical post. Nailing the feet to a block on the post or the post itself allowed the victim to support himself. As the victim hung from the crossbeam, blood could no longer circulate and the victim suffocated over the course of several days. The only relief came from supporting himself on the block, but as exhaustion set in, suffocation was inevitable.

OVERVIEW

Pilate found Jesus' claim to be King of the Jews a religious rather than a political statement and, therefore, not under Roman jurisdiction.

The chief priests added to the charges leveled against Jesus. By including charges of subverting the nation and opposing the payment of taxes, the chief priests hoped to give the matter a civil tone. The Roman authorities would have denied responsibility for a strictly religious matter.

Herod Antipas was likely in Jerusalem to celebrate the Passover feast. By recognizing Herod's jurisdiction over Jesus, Pilate showed political courtesy and passed the responsibility off to someone else.

Barabbas was a noted criminal who had been convicted of rebellion and murder. Pilate hoped to appease the crowd by giving them a choice between a man Pilate thought innocent and a man clearly a threat.

It is unlikely that the crowd on its own would have demanded Jesus' death. The chief priests, who were determined to rid themselves of the threat they thought Jesus posed, incited the crowd. In finally agreeing to their demands, Pilate became a part of the conspiracy and carried some of the guilt associated with putting an innocent man to death.

Those convicted and under the death penalty were required to carry their own crossbeam to the site of execution. Pressing another into such service likely meant the soldiers feared Jesus would die before He could be executed. By law, Roman soldiers could press anyone into service at any time.

Jesus echoed the earlier prophets when He told the women to mourn for the inhabitants of Jerusalem rather than for Him. Jerusalem would once again find itself under judgment and experience suffering as a result.

The irony of the rulers' taunting was that Jesus' death in one sense did save Him because He remained obedient to the Father's will. His death also would save others to a far greater degree than ever imagined. The irony of their taunting was similar to Satan's (4.3, 9).

Jesus' promise to the criminal that he would enjoy paradise was the ultimate act of forgiveness and mercy. The criminal had only to recognize and repent of his sin. Nothing more was required to experience God's forgiveness.

The *sixth hour* was just before noon and the *ninth hour* just before 3:00 p.m.

The veil of the temple was the curtain that separated the Holy of Holies and the sanctuary. The ripped veil exposed the place God resided and signaled the renewed access to God that occurred as a result of Jesus' sacrificial death.

The centurion's recognition of Jesus' righteousness and innocence echoed that of the criminal on the cross. Both were testimonies that Jesus was who He said He was.

The body of Jesus was wrapped in linen and laid in an unused tomb, all part of an honorable burial.

INSIGHTS

Jesus forgave his enemies. We tend to push our enemies aside. We don't identify with them and as a result, we have a hard time forgiving them. Jesus took on our identity (minus our sin) so He could forgive His enemies—us. He didn't focus on the enemy side of us, but on the image bearer side (Gen. 1.26). Forgiveness is never easy to extend and always has a cost to the forgiver. It is given with no expectation of payment from the forgiven. We are called to forgive in the same way Jesus did: down a difficult road with no cost to the recipient.

1. The leaders of the Jewish people were so focused on what they believed to be right that they completely missed the truth Jesus proclaimed. In what areas of your life is your focus so narrow you could be in danger of missing a greater truth? How can you be open minded and yet firmly planted in the Truth? How can the Holy Spirit be a guide and help in ensuring you are not unduly influenced in the wrong ways?

2. As his life reached its very last moments, one thief crucified with Jesus received reassurance he would enjoy eternal life with Jesus for doing no more than expressing his belief in Jesus. Do you believe all that is required for one to experience eternal life is expressing faith in Jesus? What would you say to someone who said eternal life requires more than just expressing faith in Jesus? What scriptures might you point to in order to back up your belief?

LUKE 24

BACKGROUND

Many of the Old Testament writers prophesied the coming of the Messiah. Jesus' life, death, and resurrection fulfilled many of these prophecies while others remain to be fulfilled during Jesus' second coming. Some of the fulfilled prophesies include: the Messiah would be a descendant of David (Jer. 23.5), He would be born of a virgin (Is. 7.14), He would enter Jerusalem on a donkey (Zech. 9.9), and He would voluntarily endure the suffering and death sinners' deserve (Is 53.7-8).

OVERVIEW

Jesus stated on several occasions that He would be killed but would rise again. The disciples did not immediately understand that Jesus' words had been fulfilled for a variety of reasons. First, rising from the dead was not a normal event. Second, the disciples' idea of the Messiah was more political in nature. They expected someone who would have enough power and authority to free them from Roman domination. Third, the testimony of women was considered unstable and undependable and needed a man's endorsement.

In the Old Testament, angels often took the form of humans and on occasion appeared in radiant clothing. Although Luke refers to the individuals at the tomb as men, they fit the Old Testament description of angels.

Peter may have been the first to begin comprehending what had really happened because he had personally experienced Jesus' prediction coming true.

The disciples traveling to Emmaus expressed the sentiment all of Jesus' followers had: the hope that the man known as Jesus who had been crucified would redeem Israel from the bondage in which she found herself. Though the disciples understood it was the third day and had heard the women's report, they did not understand the significance of what had happened until Jesus explained the (Old Testament) scriptures to them. They finally recognized Jesus when He blessed and broke the bread in a similar manner to that of the Passover meal.

Although the disciples had heard that Jesus had risen from the dead, initially seeing Him proved to be frightening. The disciples at first imagined they were seeing a ghost or apparition. Since ghosts and spirits did not have flesh and bones, and it was believed they could not eat, Jesus invited the disciples to touch Him as well as asked for something to eat to prove He was not a ghost.

Once again, Jesus opened minds to understanding so that the prophecies of His coming in the scriptures were clear to His disciples.

Before departing, Jesus summarized the reason for His life, death, and resurrection and commissioned His disciples to preach that truth to all the nations. They were not to begin, however, until they had received the Promise of the Father—the Holy Spirit.

Now understanding the truth of who Jesus was, what He had come to the world to give, and awaiting the promise of the Holy Spirit, the disciples returned to Jerusalem filled with joy.

INSIGHTS

Although Jesus promised His followers that placing their faith in Him would include persecution and suffering, He also promised they would receive the Holy Spirit, who would guide them as well as give them strength and perseverance in times of need. The same Holy Spirit guides, strengthens, and provides for all those who believe in Jesus. We must still face persecution and suffering, but we do not do it alone. The Holy Spirit is always with us and never abandons us. One of His titles is Comforter, which He readily provides as we experience the need. As with the apostles, we cannot fulfill Christ's will without the Holy Spirit.

1. Jesus' followers did not fully understand Jesus' promise that He would be resurrected after His agonizing death on the cross. As a result, they spent three days living in fear and confusion. What promises of scripture might you meditate on to gain better understanding of and thereby gain greater hope for the future? How often do you invite the Holy Spirit to reveal to you that which you do not understand or do not know? In the midst of fear and confusion, how can you create space for Jesus in order to trust that all He has said and promised will come to pass?

2. As Jesus accompanied the men on their way to Emmaus, He explained the scriptures to the men. The entire Old Testament points to the need for and coming of Jesus. Think of one or two Old Testament stories you are familiar with. How do these stories foreshadow Jesus? How are the Old and New Testaments one congruent story of God's plan of redemption for the people He loves? Can you see the scriptures as a love letter from God to you because He loves and delights in you so greatly?

ACTS

Acts, written by Luke, serves as a sequel to the Gospels. In his Gospel, Luke focused on the *life* of Jesus. In Acts, Luke focused on the *effect* of Jesus. Hope did not end when Jesus' life ended. Jesus, the resurrected Messiah, was not only alive but had sent the Holy Spirit who repeatedly convicted and encouraged people into deep heart change. Their resulting faith in the Messiah led not only to salvation and personal change but to testimonies that led others to make the same faith commitment.

Luke ended his Gospel and began Acts with Jesus' commissioning of the apostles just before He ascended to heaven. He commanded them to be witnesses in Jerusalem, Judea, and to the ends of the earth. Beginning with the apostles and continuing with the new believers, their testimonies had a ripple effect that is today still reaching out to the *ends of the earth.*

Jesus' commission serves as a rough outline for the book of Acts. First, the message was shared in Jerusalem and Judea (1.1-6.7), then it moved to Judea and Samaria (6.8-9.31), and finally to the ends of the earth (9.32-28.31).

In addition to serving as record of the effect of Jesus on the growth of the early church, Acts also serves as a historical background for a good portion of the balance of the New Testament. Of the twenty-two letters included, eleven were written during the thirty-year period Acts covers. As a result, context can be put around a letter such as Galatians by reading the events that led to Paul writing to this newly developing church body.

Luke not only recorded the historical events but several of the conflicts as well. In doing so, we have a record of how and why certain decisions affecting the worldwide church were made. For instance, the debate of whether the good news of Jesus was meant just for the Jewish people, God's chosen nation, or was intended for Jews and Gentiles alike was settled in favor of both groups. Today we continue the original apostles' understanding of Jesus' teaching by sharing the Gospel message with *all* people, excluding no one.

ACTS 1

BACKGROUND

Lots were a means of divination and were used on occasion with God's blessing. The Israelites believed that God controlled the fall of the lots, thus divinely communicating His response. There appear to be several means of casting lots, though the exact method is unknown. The use of lots to select the new apostle is the last mention of lots in the Bible. Once the Holy Spirit had been received, God communicated more directly with His people.

OVERVIEW

When writing two volume works, writers of ancient texts would often repeat the final verses of the first text in the beginning verses of the second text. The repetition would not necessarily be recorded word for word. Rather, the general points could appear in different wording. Readers of these ancient texts would have assumed these differences were for the sake of readability rather than the result of oversight or error.

Luke addressed his account to the same person as his first book: Theophilus, of whom nothing is known.

Jesus' promise of the coming Holy Spirit prompted questions about His coming kingdom, which was expected to come at the same time the Messiah came. Jesus assured them that the promised kingdom would indeed come, but only the Father knew the time or season in which the event would occur. In the meantime, the disciples could count on the power of the Holy Spirit to accomplish all Jesus was sending them to do.

Time referred to how long, while seasons referred to *events* that took place within time. In effect, Jesus told his disciples no one but the Father knew how long until the coming of the kingdom, nor what events would transpire during the passage of that time.

The Messiah was expected to come to the Mount of Olives (Zech. 14.4).

A *Sabbath day's journey* was the distance (about half a mile) one was allowed to walk under Jewish law on the Sabbath without breaking the fourth commandment (work for six days, rest on the seventh).

The women's inclusion with the group of men is significant. Women of the time were generally marginalized. Here they appear to be equals with the men.

While Peter, James, and John are mentioned throughout Acts and several other New Testament books, the balance of the apostles are named here for the last time.

Since Judas had betrayed Jesus and was no longer eligible to be an apostle, a replacement was sought. Peter specified two qualifications. First, the man had to have been with the group since Jesus' baptism by John (the beginning of Jesus' ministry) and second, he had to have witnessed the resurrection. Both these specifications meant the new apostle would have been an eyewitness of all the events of Jesus' ministry. He would, therefore, have the same authority as the other apostles and offer the same eyewitness accounts during the critical first days of the early church.

INSIGHTS

Jesus' final words to His disciples commissioned them to carry the good news to Jerusalem, Judah, Samaria, and the ends of the earth. Though tradition holds that ten of the eleven apostles died as martyrs, they were all empowered to be witnesses despite the opposition they experienced. Jesus' commission has been passed down through the ages and today rests on all believers. Our task is not to convince people, but to share the truth of the gospel. God will empower us, as He did the disciples, despite opposition we may face.

1. Jesus asked the disciples to stay in Jerusalem until they received the promise of the Father. They obediently waited and did not press forward on their own. Do you wait in obedience when Jesus asks you to stay or do you move ahead without Him?

2. The disciples were quick to pray for instruction regarding a replacement for Judas. How well do you seek God's direction before you make decisions?

ACTS 2

BACKGROUND

Pentecost was one of three major feasts celebrated by the Jewish people. The other two were Passover and the Feast of Tabernacles. Pentecost (Greek for *fifty*) occurred fifty days after the Sabbath of Passover. It is also referred to as the *Feast of Weeks* and the *Feast of Harvest*. Pentecost was a celebration of the harvest and the firstfruits were brought to the temple in thanksgiving for God's provision and for His blessing on the remainder of the harvest.

OVERVIEW

It was no coincidence that the Holy Spirit came on Pentecost. His coming represented the firstfruits of Christ's church and the beginning of the *harvest* of souls.

The term *tongues* is the Greek word for known languages. The Holy Spirit gave those on whom He descended the ability to speak in languages previously unknown to them. Passover attracted pilgrims from many foreign countries, many of whom stayed until Pentecost. Those newly baptized in the Holy Spirit now had the ability to share the good news of Christ with many more people than they would have otherwise.

At the Tower of Babel, God judged the people and made their languages unintelligible to each other (Gen. 11.9). Here the reverse occurs. With the coming of the Holy Spirit, people communicated with those for whom there had previously been a language barrier.

Peter refuted the allegation that he and the rest of the disciples had been drinking so early in the day. The third hour of the day would have been 9:00 in the morning. In addition, Jews would have abstained from eating and drinking on holy days until later in the day.

Peter, the first to recognize Jesus as the Messiah, was the first to testify to (preach) the good news of Christ.

In Old Testament times, God's Spirit had been given to specific people for a predefined period of time. Joel's writings contain a prophecy that God's Spirit would be poured out on all believers (Joel 2.28-32). Peter quoted the passage and stated that it had been fulfilled.

Peter applied logic as he argued his case. Joel had prophesied that the Spirit would be sent. Jesus had fulfilled that prophecy when He sent the Spirit. Since He could not have sent the Spirit if He were dead, He must be alive. In addition, Jesus could only have sent the Spirit if He had ascended to heaven. Peter's second quote came from Psalm 16.8-11 in which David said the Messiah or Holy One would be incorruptible (not decaying). David himself had died and was buried in a tomb that was undisputedly his. Therefore, David could not have been speaking about himself but about one of his descendants. Jesus was that descendant. It was true He had been crucified, died, and buried, but it was equally true He had been resurrected, seen by the disciples, and ascended to sit at the right hand of God (Psalm 110.1, Peter's final quote). As a result of these points, Jesus had to be both God and Messiah.

Such a large group carried with it a responsibility to train new believers. They were instructed in the teachings of Jesus, brought into fellowship with other believers, partook in the breaking of bread (likely the Lord's Supper, though some have asserted this had broader implications in the early church), and educated in the discipline of prayer.

INSIGHTS

Just as new believers received training in the early church, so it is important today for all believers, new and veteran, to receive the same type of training. Without knowledge of the teachings of Jesus, believers risk falling away from their new faith due to the deceitful lies of the enemy. Fellowship provides an opportunity for encouragement and admonishment while celebrating the Lord's Supper not only fulfills Jesus' command to do so but also serves as a reminder of His sacrifice on our behalf. Finally, prayer is essential to the life of believers as it serves as one means of communicating with God.

1. The sending of the Holy Spirit was a gift from Jesus (v.38). Why do you think sending the Spirit was so important to Jesus? Why is He important to us as believers today?

2. Why did Peter refer back to the prophets of old as part of his argument for convincing the Jews of the truth of Jesus as Messiah? Why is looking back to the prophets' words about Jesus important for us as modern day believers?

3. The new believers *devoted themselves to the apostles' teaching and to the fellowship, to the breaking of bread and to prayer* (2.42). These four practices form the foundation for a strong and godly faith. How often do you engage in each practice? Are there any adjustments you need to make to engage in one or more of these practices on a more regular basis?

Acts 3

BACKGROUND

The *Beautiful Gate* is believed to be an alternate name for the Nicanor Gate (named after its donor), which led from the Court of Women into the Temple. The east-facing gate was made of bronze and is thought to have shimmered beautifully in the glow of the rising sun. Neither women nor those disfigured in any manner were allowed into the Temple. There were fifteen steps that led to the gate and they were regularly filled with those seeking alms.

OVERVIEW

Peter was clear that what was about to happen was not done in the power the apostles possessed but by the power of the name of Jesus Christ.

The beggar responded in a manner that reflected his joy: leaping, walking, and praising the one who had made his healing possible. As a maimed individual, the beggar had been excluded from Temple worship since the time of his birth. Entering the Temple after being healed was therefore the first time he had ever done so.

The porch or portico named *Solomon's* may have survived from Solomon's temple.

One ancient belief was that very pious people were able to perform miracles by getting God to pay attention to them. Peter made it clear that he and his companions were ordinary people empowered by God's Spirit.

Luke's report of Peter's speech contains some irony. Jesus, the prince or author of life was killed in exchange for a murderer.

Peter acknowledged that the people called for Jesus' death out of ignorance, but such justification did not excuse them from the guilt of sin (Hos. 4.6).

INSIGHTS

After healing the beggar, Peter stated that the Jews and Romans were responsible for Jesus' death, and His death served the eternal plans of God. His statement is analogous to Joseph's words when his brothers sought forgiveness for what they had done. He assured them that what they had meant for evil, God had used for good (Gen. 50.20). Even today, God is able to use the wicked things men do to bring about His eternal plan. In so doing, God sometimes redeems the wicked things we have done and other times uses the evil done to us to bring about good. In either case, we can rejoice in God's mercy and blessing.

1. After the beggar was healed, he began walking, jumping, and praising God! How do you praise God for His goodness toward you each day?

2. Peter again summed up the story of Jesus' death for the listeners with a plea to repent and turn to God. Have you received Jesus as your personal Savior? If not, take this time to repent, receive His forgiveness and gift of the Holy Spirit, and turn your life towards God. He is waiting in excitement for you! If you have just received Jesus as your Savior, whom can you share your commitment with?

Acts 4

BACKGROUND

The Sadducees had primary responsibility for administration of the Temple. They did not regard as true the Pharisees' belief in the resurrection of the dead. Conflict between the Sadducees and Pharisees over this and other differences had existed for some time. Eyewitness testimony to a resurrection would have severely threatened the authority of the Sadducees and their position in the Temple.

OVERVIEW

Peter and John arrived for prayer about the ninth hour, or 3:00 p.m., and healed the lame man. It would have been late afternoon by the time they were confronted by the Sadducees. Since evening trials were illegal and the priests were no longer dealing with just one man, Peter and John were held overnight to appear before the gathering of priests and other religious officials (known as the Sanhedrin) the next day.

Annas was high priest until A.D. 14 when the Romans removed him from the position. The Jewish people viewed their religion as a national matter and, therefore, did not recognize the authority of the Romans to remove Annas from his position. Caiaphas, Annas' son-in-law, was the actual high priest at the time. John (not John the apostle) is thought to be Annas' son and assumed the position of high priest in A.D. 37.

Jesus was the first to state that He was the fulfillment of Psalm 118.22. Peter repeated the assertion as a defense for his teaching.

No one could dispute that the lame man had been healed, so the dispute centered on the authority under which the man had been healed.

Scholars disagree on precisely what raising their voice in *one accord* means. Most believe it meant the people were in agreement as they worshipped God while a few believe it meant the people spoke in unison.

The worship leader quoted from both Psalm 146.6 and Psalm 2.1-2. The focus of the prayer was that God would give the people boldness to continue speaking His word despite the threats they had received from the religious leaders.

For the early church, *being filled with the Holy Spirit* went beyond proclaiming the Word of God and included sharing what they had with those in need.

Levites in Old Testament times did not own land, but by the time of Jesus, some did.

Though the chapter breaks in the middle, Luke contrasted a positive with a negative in the area of giving. Such contrast was a recommended technique in ancient writing.

Neither God nor the apostles demanded that the people give over all their property. As people came to believe in Jesus and were filled with the Holy Spirit, their change in heart led them to share God's concerns in a much deeper manner. One of those concerns was for those who were in need.

INSIGHTS

Peter's statement about choosing whether to listen to God or man is very relevant to us today. There are many forces in the United States as well as around the world that are desperately trying to silence the good news of Jesus Christ. Laws are passed forbidding prayer in schools, banning displays of the 10 Commandments, and redefining marriage. Though we may suffer in the short term, we are *always* better off following God in the long term. It is too easy to be duped by the world and even ourselves into believing God has said something He has not. The key is knowing with certainty what God says. Such certainty can be gained by reading the Bible on a regular basis.

1. Peter was always quick to give Jesus the credit for the power in his life. Are you able to see the power Jesus gives you daily? Do you give Jesus credit? Are you thankful for what He does on your behalf?

2. The early believers shared all they had to ensure there was no needy person among them. How generous are you? Do you tend to hold your possessions tightly or loosely? Are you quick to share with others, especially other believers, when needs arise?

3. In Verse 29 the believers pray for the ability to speak the Word with great boldness. What a great prayer! How boldly do you speak to those with questions about the Christian faith or who oppose it? Is praying for boldness something you could or should add to your prayers? If you struggle with speaking boldly when the opportunities arise, what holds you back?

Acts 5

BACKGROUND

Ananias and Sapphira were not the first to be severely punished for being deceitful before God. Achan hid some of the spoils for his personal use that were to be dedicated to God. His dishonesty cost the lives of both him and his family (Josh. 7). King Saul also attempted to deceive God by holding onto plunder that was to be sacrificed to God. Saul's decision cost him his right to serve as Israel's king (1 Sam. 15).

OVERVIEW

Ananias and Sapphira's sin was not that they desired to keep a part of the proceeds from the sale of their land for themselves. They sinned because they gave the impression they were donating the entire proceeds to the needs of the church. In other words, they lied to the apostles and, more grievously, to God.

Peter first stated Ananias lied to the Holy Spirit (v. 3), then that he lied to God (v. 4). Since the Holy Spirit is part of the Godhead, lying to the Holy Spirit is the same as lying to God.

The judgment Ananias and Sapphira received for their deceitfulness may seem severe; however, it was critical to the growth of the young church that it not suffer spiritual damage. The fear that resulted ensured the new believers acted with honesty and integrity.

In ancient times, a person's shadow was thought to be connected to the person. As a result, people placed great hope in Peter's shadow falling on them.

The release from prison contains action on the parts of both God and the apostles. First the angel *opened and brought*, then the apostles were commanded to *go, stand,* and *speak*. God did not release the apostles from prison in order that they might be safe, but rather that they might continue to preach His word.

Gamaliel was a well-known Pharisee and a part of the aristocracy in Jerusalem. He also served as a teacher to Saul (later Paul; 22.3).

In general, Pharisees did not believe in executing someone because of his/her political beliefs. As a result, Gamaliel warned the Sanhedrin to be careful. In the past, those who claimed to be someone important had influenced a number of people, but only for as long as they were alive. Once they died, the people dispersed and no longer posed a threat. Gamaliel believed the same would happen with the followers of Jesus if Jesus, in fact, proved to be inconsequential. However, if Jesus was who He said He was and the Sanhedrin continued trying to prevent His followers from teaching His truth, they would be fighting against God Himself.

The Sanhedrin released the apostles after administering physical punishment. This is the first instance of persecution suffered by Christian believers.

Jesus had experienced suffering in order to accomplish God's will. The apostles rejoiced that God counted them worthy to also experience suffering in bringing about His will. In so doing, the apostles set a precedent for the persecution and suffering later Christians, including Christians today, would and do experience.

INSIGHTS

The apostles were released from prison and instructed to return to the place where they had been arrested in order to continue doing God's work. In the same way, God often will protect us, not that we might be safe, but that we might continue to take risks on His behalf. It has been said that we are far better off being in God's will (i.e. obediently doing as He directs) in a place of danger, than outside God's will in a place of safety. In addition, deep joy and fulfillment come from using what God has given us in order to do the work He has called us to do.

1. Ananias and Sapphira were put to death for keeping a portion of the money for themselves. It was not sinful to keep the money, but it was sinful to make it appear as though they had given all they earned. What things do you hold back from God? How do you make yourself appear before men versus God? Are you living a life of integrity?

2. Though Peter and the apostles had been instructed not to teach in Jesus' name, they continued to do so, even after being thrown into prison for violating the order. Though the high priest was indignant and threatening, Peter was sure of his response. He was certain his obedience belonged to God and not to men. When faced with temptations to compromise your faith, are you as confident about where your obedience belongs? What might you need to do to increase your confidence? In the face of threats and persecution, how can you have the same confidence Peter had?

Acts 6

BACKGROUND

By the time of Jesus, there were thousands of priests in Israel. Though some were upper class Sadducees and Pharisees, the vast majority were poorer priests who served in the Temple only a few weeks out of the year. Their conversion to Christianity would have been particularly threatening as they represented a significant inroad into the Temple itself.

OVERVIEW

The Hellenists were Jews who had lived outside of Israel. They were raised in a primarily Greek culture, spoke Greek as their native language, and used the Septuagint, the Greek translation of the Old Testament scriptures. The Hebrews spoke Aramaic as their native language, though many also spoke Greek, and used the Hebrew Old Testament.

Care of those who could not provide for themselves, especially widows and orphans, was an important Old Testament teaching. Animosity may have arisen between the Hellenists and the Hebrews, causing some of the widows to be neglected.

The apostles did not assign blame but looked for a solution to the issue. They recognized their own inability to meet all the needs of the new believers, and so determined to assign responsibility to others. Three criteria were established for the selection of the men: they had to have a good reputation, be filled with the Holy Spirit, and be men of wisdom. These items would have shown a consistency between their profession of faith and the way in which they lived their lives. All seven of the men chosen had Greek names, suggesting they were immigrants and part of the offended minority.

The seven men were already *filled with the Holy Spirit*, so when the apostles laid hands on them it was not to receive what they already had. Instead, it was used here and in the Old Testament (Num. 8.10; 27.18) to commission or confer ministry responsibility upon an individual.

The Jewish law of rebuke required a warning be issued before action could be taken. Since the Sanhedrin had already warned the leaders of the new movement, they were prepared to take immediate action with Stephen.

The message Stephen preached would have made the Temple as the central place of worship no longer relevant and was, therefore, a great threat to the established religious authorities.

Synagogues were local places of worship, scripture reading, instruction in the Law of Moses, and community centers. They often served as courts where local justice was administered and elementary schools where children were taught to read. Hellenistic Jews from outside Jerusalem used the Synagogue of Freedom. Fearful of the repercussions that might arise if Stephen continued to preach the message of Jesus, the leaders of the synagogue induced men to state that Stephen had spoken blasphemously against Moses and God. According to Jewish law, blasphemy was punishable by death although, under Roman law, the Jews could not execute anyone.

INSIGHTS

One of the natural outcomes of newfound faith in Jesus Christ is a desire to share Him with others. Often, people feel a great release from the burden of sin and a freedom they have never known before. They cannot help but want those around them to experience the same release and freedom. In this manner, the early church was able to fulfill Jesus' command and spread the Word of God. And in like manner, we too can fulfill Jesus' command to spread His good news to the ends of the earth. Inviting people to know Christ does not require a college degree or other special training. Instead, we need simply share with others what Jesus has done for us.

1. When the disciples were unable to meet the needs of the widows, we see the beginning of what we today call a ministry as they put together a group of men to find a solution to the problem. Have you experienced any needs being met through ministry? Are you participating in a ministry yourself? If not, would you pray about where God would want to use you to further His kingdom?

2. Stephen, a faithful follower of Jesus, faced false accusations for speaking the truth about Jesus. Have you ever been falsely accused of something? How did you respond? Were you able to respond in faith as Stephen did? Did you trust God through the experience? How might you respond differently the next time you face false accusations and persecution?

ACTS 7

BACKGROUND

Stephen's scriptural references came from the Septuagint (the Greek translation of the Old Testament), which differed slightly from the Hebrew version of the Old Testament. The differences between the two tend to be minor; however, they can be noticeable when what Stephen said is compared to the Hebrew version of the Old Testament (from which the English translations are derived). For instance, Stephen stated seventy-five people accompanied Jacob to Egypt while the Hebrew states the number was sixty-six.

OVERVIEW

Reciting Jewish history was a common method of making points. Stephen's recitation of God's interaction with His people pointed to Stephen's contention that neither the Temple nor the land was central to God's plan of salvation for His people. He also alleged that Jesus was the final man of God who was rejected by the people He was sent to deliver. Stephen quoted the Old Testament extensively and presented a logical, point-by-point argument to prove his premise.

Abraham received the promise of the land in Mesopotamia, far from the land his descendants would one day possess.

Stephen's second point centered on the contention that Joseph was a man of God who had been rejected by most of the patriarchs (ten of his eleven brothers). Those patriarchs were the ancestors of most of the Jewish people. As descendants, the current leaders had carried on the tradition of rejecting God's chosen when they crucified Jesus.

Stephen next cited the story of Moses to reiterate that God revealed Himself outside the land of Israel and that the people continued to reject their deliverers. He included the story of the burning bush to show that God reveals Himself in ways He chooses and anywhere God reveals Himself becomes holy ground.

Stephen contended that although God had given Moses the instructions for building the tabernacle, which was then built according to specifications and God's presence was in the tabernacle, He could never be confined to something made by those whom He Himself had made. God had not intended for the Temple to be worshipped as an idol because His presence dwelled there. Instead, the Temple was to be a place in which the people could connect with God.

Stephen quoted Amos and Isaiah and contended their messages were just as relevant for the people of his own time as they had been for the people of the prophets' time.

Though Stephen's speech was made because he was defending himself in front of the Sanhedrin, he was more focused on convincing his listeners to recognize the rightful claim of Jesus.

Stephen used very direct and insulting language in his final statement. *Stiff-necked* and *uncircumcised of heart* were used repeatedly by the Old Testament prophets to point to the people's stubbornness, determination to make their own rules, and lack of obedience to God. In doing so, Stephen drove home the point that his listeners had rejected God's messengers just as their ancestors had.

Stephen's reward for speaking the truth that would very shortly cost him his life was a glorious vision of Jesus.

Under Roman law, subject people could not engage in carrying out capital punishment, but Stephen's listeners were so enraged by what they heard, they ignored Roman law and executed him under their own Jewish law.

INSIGHTS

Looking death in the face can be a terrifying experience, but just as

Stephen quickly realized, looking past death into the face of Jesus brings a hope that dissipates all fear. Today, we may not be blessed with a vision similar to Stephen's, but we can face our own or a loved one's impending death with great hope when we can claim with confidence the eternal life God promises to all who believe in Him. That eternal life, when we rule and reign with God, will be far better than anything we experience in this life.

1. Stephen gave the Sanhedrin a summary of the history of God's people up to the current times. Do you take the time to review your history with God? Have you looked back over your lifetime and seen how God has been a present force? If the need arose, could you give a brief statement about how and why God sent His Son to live, die, and rise from the dead?

2. Stephen, the first Christian martyr, willingly gave up his life for his faith in Jesus. How far do you think you are willing to go? How do you respond to persecution? What might you do to increase your faith and confidence in Jesus so you can stand strong in the face of persecution?

Acts 8

BACKGROUND

Saul would later be known as Paul, the apostle, after he experienced a dramatic meeting with the resurrected Jesus Christ (9.1-20). Though he fully supported Stephen's execution (22.20), he also acknowledged that God was able to bring about His purpose and plan through the events that were actually designed to thwart His aims (Rom. 8.28).

The word *simony* means the buying and selling of church privileges or offices and came from the practices of Simon.

OVERVIEW

Being left unburied after death was considered a great dishonor, though it was a common outcome for criminals. Stephen's friends ignored the ruling made by the council and honored Stephen with a proper burial.

The judgment against Stephen began wider persecution against the young Christian church. The primary leader of the attack appears to have been Saul, who imprisoned women as well as men. It was unusual for women to be imprisoned in these circumstances and points to the zealousness with which Saul acted.

The persecution prompted many to flee and take the good news with them. While the persecution was meant to stop the spread of the new religion, it actually caused the church to do what Jesus had commanded.

Philip was the second of the seven newly commissioned men Luke highlighted. As he preached the message of Jesus and performed miracles, he attracted many who believed.

Given the animosity that existed between Jews and Samaritans, the response to Philip, a Jew, was remarkable and served as a witness to the power of the Holy Spirit.

Though Simon had professed faith in Jesus and was baptized, he interpreted what he saw in the new religion by his old beliefs. It was common for magicians in ancient times to buy and sell magical formulas. Simon thought the Holy Spirit was another such formula that could easily be bought for the right price.

God set up a divine appointment for Philip with the Ethiopian eunuch. Since Samaritans were considered half-breeds, the Ethiopian is often considered the first Gentile convert. He was also the first to take the Gospel message to the *ends of the earth.*

During this period most people traveled by foot. Wealthier members of society often traveled on animals. The chariot and at least one attendant the eunuch traveled with are an indication of his high status.

The eunuch was reading from Isaiah 53 (though the scriptures did not have chapter and verse references until many centuries later). This passage spoke of the suffering servant. The Jewish people of the time believed the Messiah would come as a delivering King with mighty power to overthrow Israel's oppressors. In this thought pattern, the suffering servant was viewed as the suffering nation of Israel. Philip revealed that the suffering Servant was actually Jesus, who had died on the cross for the sins of all humanity.

Baptism is the outward sign of a person's decision to follow Christ. Conveniently, God provided water in the desert in which the eunuch could be baptized.

Scholars have debated what is actually meant by the Lord suddenly taking Philip away. Some believe he was miraculously transported to another location while others believe the Holy Spirit suddenly led him away.

INSIGHTS

Just as Simon became a believer in the new faith but hung on to his old and inaccurate beliefs, so we, too, can place our faith in Christ, while trying to fit the new faith into our old thought patterns. In some cases, these old inaccuracies slightly color our understanding of Jesus and His teachings. In other cases, they can completely hinder our growth and maturity in the faith. As a result, it is important to seek to understand the scriptures as God intends us to understand them, not as we might rationalize them. We can do this by seeking the guidance of the Holy Spirit, praying for understanding, and learning from solid Biblical teachers.

1. Even though Stephen's death was a tragedy, God was ultimately glorified because it forced the believers to scatter, allowing for the spread of the gospel throughout the world. In your own life, can you see how things that seem to be tragedies can actually be God at work in your life or in the lives of those around you? How was your faith strengthened or the gospel spread because of such a tragedy?

2. Both Simon the sorcerer and the Ethiopian eunuch were curious about Jesus, yet had very different hearts towards God. Their contrasting responses to the good news remind us that when our hearts are open, God is eager to reveal Himself. Where is your heart toward God? Is it full of bitterness and captive to sin, as Simon's was, or is it open and ready to receive all that He has to give, as the eunuch's was?

Acts 9

BACKGROUND

Straight Street ran from east to west across the entire city of ancient Damascus. Today it is still possible to see the house traditionally held to be Judas'.

Saul was not the first to escape an attempt on his life by fleeing over a city wall. Rahab helped the spies in Jericho (Josh. 2.15) and David fled Saul with Michal's help (1 Sam. 19.12).

Joppa is modern day Jaffa. It is located adjacent to Tel Aviv and is still an important port city on the Mediterranean.

OVERVIEW

Those who followed Jesus were originally called *disciples* or *followers of the Way.*

At this time, Roman authorities allowed the Sanhedrin to govern Jewish religious affairs. As a result, the Sanhedrin had authority over synagogues in distant, even Gentile, cities. The letters Saul requested were documents that gave him permission to arrest anyone who followed after Jesus. Damascus was located about 140 miles northeast of Jerusalem.

In an effort to keep the new religion from spreading, Saul's intent was to track down followers of Jesus who had fled the persecution in Jerusalem.

Some translations include a verse in which Jesus states it was hard for Saul to *kick against goads*. Stephen's final speech and the explosion of new believers were an annoyance (goad) Saul tried to suppress. He did not recognize these were actually the result of promptings of the Holy Spirit.

Two other men named Ananias are mentioned in Acts, but it was a common name of the time and there was no relation between the three men. Nothing is known of the Ananias God sent to Saul. He was a disciple (not an apostle) and may have come to faith by following Jesus during His lifetime or may have been a newer believer.

Saul's previous training would have made him an expert in the scriptures. Once his eyes were opened to Jesus and His role as Messiah, Paul would have quickly been able to understand the scriptures in a new light. He then went on to preach from his newly gained understanding.

Although Saul had not had the opportunity to carry out his plans in Damascus, rumors were likely circulating as to what he intended to do. The believers in Damascus would, therefore, have been astonished at Saul's change of heart. Such change was not enough to convince the religious leaders, who had the same reaction to Saul as others had to Stephen. In effect, Saul picked up where Stephen left off.

Tarsus, Saul's hometown, was located about three hundred miles north of Jerusalem and ten miles inland from the Mediterranean Sea.

The churches had peace because Paul was no longer focused on persecuting the followers of Jesus. In addition, the new emperor of Rome, Caligula, wanted to erect a statue of himself in the Jerusalem Temple. Jewish attention was more focused on preventing this than suppressing the new religion.

The physical healing of Aeneas led to many spiritual healings as people saw evidence of the truth of Jesus' message.

Peter's healing of Tabitha was very similar to Jesus' healing of Jairus' daughter (Luke 8.54). In addition to similar settings, Jesus would have said *Talitha cumi* (Aramaic for *little girl, arise*) while Peter said *Tabitha cumi*, a difference of only one letter.

INSIGHTS

Ananias was willing to do as the Lord called but was hesitant when he realized to whom God was sending him. We, too, may be called to do something that seems unbelievable. It may be to confront someone who has caused us great pain, speak to a person who seems beyond redemption, or rebuke a vocal critic of all that is ungodly. Though we may initially question what we heard, our response needs to be the same as Ananias'—obedience. Just as the fearful persecutor, Saul, received Jesus and was baptized, so we may well see similar dramatic results when we obey God's command to go.

1. Saul was perhaps the most unlikely of converts. He was intent on wiping out the new belief in Jesus sweeping through the country by whatever means he could use. Yet God had a grand plan for Saul's life. Do you know that God has a plan for all believers? Do you believe God has a plan for your life? Are you living out that plan? If not, what are one or two steps you could take to gain a greater understanding of God's plan for your life?

2. While in Joppa, Peter stayed with a tanner named Simon. Tanners were frequently in contact with dead animals, making them ritually unclean on a regular basis and therefore people Jews would have avoided. Peter's willingness to stay with Simon shows how his perceptions were changing as his faith grew. In what areas of your life do you hold prejudices? Are there ideas, beliefs, or values you need to let go of in order to more fully live out your faith? Have you asked God to change your heart in the areas that need changing?

Acts 10

BACKGROUND

Chapter 10 is a turning point in Acts. Up to this point, the new believers had witnessed primarily to their Jewish countrymen. Luke now begins recounting the promptings of the Holy Spirit that lead the believers to reach out to the Gentiles.

OVERVIEW

Cornelius was a Gentile. His position as centurion also indicates he was a Roman citizen (non-citizens could not join the regular Roman army but were permitted to serve in the auxiliary troops). Cornelius worshipped the Jewish God but likely had not converted by being circumcised.

The ninth hour was 3:00 p.m., while the sixth hour would have been noon.

From childhood, Jews were taught never to eat any animal that was unclean (Lev. 11). While Jews were lax in observing many parts of the law, they generally were quite strict about observing these dietary laws. As a result, the idea of eating what was considered unclean would have been repulsive. God repeated His command three times in order to instill its importance to Peter. The immediate context may have been difficult to comprehend, but the broader allusion would quickly become apparent. Just as God had determined what was unclean to eat and lifted the restriction, so He was redefining who were called to be His people. Gentiles would no longer be *unclean* and would be on equal ground with Jews before God.

Caesarea is about 30 miles north of Joppa. The journey would have taken a good day or longer to complete on foot.

Peter's vision was quickly put into practice when he entered Cornelius' house, a house he previously would have avoided.

Fasting was a Jewish custom that Cornelius chose to follow.

Peter recounted the life of Jesus and concluded by stating that one need only believe in the One to whom the prophets witnessed in order to receive forgiveness of their sins.

The faith of Peter's listeners was confirmed by the Holy Spirit who fell on the Gentiles in the same manner He fell upon the disciples on Pentecost. Those who traveled with Peter were astonished to see what they had not expected—God's equal acceptance of Gentile believers.

INSIGHTS

Peter had spent his entire life obeying the dietary laws that forbid eating unclean animals. God's new revelation that unclean animals could be eaten and its analogy to the Gentiles as now being considered *clean* by God would have been startling. God may also challenge our beliefs in equally startling ways. When such moments occur, we have two choices. We can ignore God and stubbornly hang on to our erroneous beliefs. Or we can respond as Peter did by trusting that God's plan will be accomplished by relinquishing our old beliefs and adopting God's revealed truth.

1. Peter and Cornelius needed each other to understand God more; Peter to know the gospel was intended for an audience much broader than the Jews, and Cornelius to know the salvation of Christ. Who are the people in your life that meet a need in your Christian faith? For whom do you meet a need?

2. The Spirit revealed to Peter that he could not call unclean that which God had made. God was so adamant Peter understand what he was saying that He repeated it three times. What areas of your life and beliefs might the Holy Spirit be trying to bring to your attention? Are there areas in which you are resisting God's efforts to change your perceptions? How can you cooperate, as Peter did, with God's efforts to show you where you need a change of heart?

Acts 11

BACKGROUND

Antioch was a very cosmopolitan city and attracted people from many different ethnic backgrounds and cultures. Because people from as far away as India and China resided in Antioch, it had tremendous potential for spreading the gospel to other parts of the world. In addition, its cultural diversity suppressed the domination of one religion over another, thereby creating an environment in which people were more open to hearing the truth of Christ's message.

OVERVIEW

Those of the circumcision were Jews who professed faith in Christ.

The Hebrew word signifying how the believers approached Peter is translated variously as *contended*, *criticized*, and *took issue with*. Though not as clear in English, the Hebrew states that the interaction was along the lines of an intense quarrel.

The believers in Jerusalem did not object to Peter's interaction with the Gentiles in Caesarea, nor that Peter shared the message of Christ with them. The believers' objection centered on the meal Peter shared with the Gentiles, who were ritually unclean. Just as eating unclean animals was forbidden by Jewish law, so was eating with unclean people.

Peter appears to have anticipated the argument he would face on his return to Jerusalem and took six *brothers* (fellow Jews) with him.

As Peter recounted what had happened with Cornelius, he made clear that the climax of God's earlier vision occurred as Peter was preaching to Cornelius and his household. Before Peter was able to finish, the Holy Spirit fell upon the Gentiles as He had come upon the disciples *at the beginning* (Pentecost).

The Jewish people believed that as God's chosen people they had been granted salvation through His sovereign grace. They believed Gentiles could also experience salvation, but they had to first convert to Judaism and be circumcised or live righteously and keep the seven laws tradition held God gave Noah. It wasn't until Peter's interaction with Cornelius that the people began to understand God's plan to offer salvation to the Gentiles on the same terms the Jewish people received His salvation.

Barnabas (meaning *son of encouragement*) lived up to his name when the believers in Jerusalem sent him out to Antioch. In addition, Barnabas traveled approximately two hundred miles round trip in order to encourage Saul and bring him back to help with the growth of the church in Antioch.

The term *Christian* was likely originally used in a derogatory manner to point out those who preached the message of Christ. The early believers called themselves *disciples, believers, saints,* or *brethren.* It was not until sometime in the second century that followers of Christ adopted the title for themselves.

The famine prophesied by Agabus became a reality. Several bad harvests and famine throughout the Roman Empire are mentioned in numerous extra-biblical records. The food shortage affected different areas in different degrees and thus provided an opportunity for the church in Antioch to offer assistance to the believers in Judea.

INSIGHTS

It can be tempting to require those desiring to place their faith in Christ to jump through a series of hoops before welcoming them as new members of the body of Christ. God made it clear to Peter that all that was required for Him to welcome a new believer was faith in His Son, Jesus. When we are tempted to require the *hoop jumping* it would serve us well to remember Peter's vision and God's determination that faith is all that is required; no more and no less.

1. God sent Peter to Cornelius to bring a message through which his household would be saved. Who did God put in your life to bring about your salvation? With whom might God be calling you to share the hope of salvation?

2. When the Holy Spirit revealed the coming famine to Agabus, the disciples responded by contributing to perhaps the first relief fund in order to aid their fellow Christian brothers and sisters. Each disciple contributed according to his ability. How do you respond when the Holy Spirit reveals a need to you? Do you prayerfully consider what part of meeting that need you can fulfill? Would you say you have a generous spirit when it comes to your possessions and time? If not, what keeps you from being generous?

Acts 12

BACKGROUND

The Herod mentioned here was Agrippa I. He was the nephew of Herod Antipas, who had John the Baptist killed, and grandson of Herod the Great, who had the Jewish male children in Bethlehem killed in an attempt to eliminate the newborn Jewish king—Jesus.

OVERVIEW

The Jewish leaders resented Herod Agrippa because he was an Edomite, rather than a Jew. Herod knew this and attempted to win their favor by killing prominent members of the newly emerging religion. James was the first of the apostles to be killed and the only one mentioned in the New Testament.

Peter was slated for execution as James had been, but this was delayed because it was against Jewish law to have a trial or sentencing during a Passover celebration.

Peter was heavily guarded to ensure he did not escape a second time (5.18-19). The sixteen soldiers would have worked three-hour shifts. It was not uncommon for a prisoner to be chained between two guards to ensure he did not escape.

James was a common name, and the James whom Peter wanted informed would have been the brother of Jesus.

The only way for Peter to have humanly escaped was for the guards to have allowed him to do so. Therefore, Herod examined the guards to determine what they knew and why they had let Peter go. But the guards had no information, so Herod chose to enact the customary penalty when a guard's prisoner escaped: the guard(s) received the sentence the prisoner was to have served. In this case, the guards were executed.

The reason for Herod's anger toward the people of Tyre and Sidon is unknown. The two cities were dependent on Herod's territories for food supplies.

Josephus, a first-century Jewish historian, recorded Herod's death occurring in nearly the exact same fashion as mentioned here in Acts, although Josephus did not attribute Herod's death to being smitten by an angel. The people attempted to appease Herod by praising him as a god and more than a man. Instead of deflecting their veneration, Herod enjoyed it. His gratification did not last long because he collapsed, was carried to his palace, and died five days later.

INSIGHTS

Though it is not recorded, the believers likely prayed as fervently for James' release as they had for Peter's. God does not reveal why He chose to release Peter but allowed James to die. Believers of James and Peter's day could only trust that God had a purpose and His plan was being accomplished. Today, believers often face a similar opportunity to trust God. We may not understand why a child is allowed to die at a very tender age or why an evil dictator lives a long life. God in His sovereignty has allowed these things, and we can only trust that His wisdom is unfailing and His purposes are being accomplished.

1. The early church's earnest prayers for Peter's release were answered in a dramatic fashion. When was the last time you earnestly prayed for someone in trouble? Do you pray with the expectation that God will work in some manner? Or do you tend to pray with little conviction? How might God be calling you to pray with greater confidence that He answers prayers?

2. Herod was put to death because of his arrogance toward God. Where is your heart and attitude with regard to your place before God? Are there any areas of your life where you have responded with pride rather than humility that you need to ask God's forgiveness for? If so, take a moment now to confess, repent, and receive God's forgiveness.

ACTS 13

BACKGROUND

A *tetrarch* was a ruler of one of four divisions of a province or country. Herod the tetrarch was also known as Herod Antipas.

Slaves were sometimes raised in the same household as a master's son. Later when the son inherited his father's possession, he often freed the slaves who had been his childhood playmates. The former slaves frequently maintained a prominent position in the household for as long as the son retained his authority.

OVERVIEW

In the early church, prophets served as God's mouthpiece by proclaiming His revelation. Teachers made the proclamations relevant to the people by explaining what they meant and how they applied to the people's lives.

According to Luke, Sergius Paulus was the first Roman ruler to believe the gospel message. Unlike Cornelius, he is presented as a pagan who had no inclination toward Judaism or Christianity. He was amazed at what he saw and believed the truth Paul shared with him.

For the first time, Luke mentions Saul's Roman name—Paul. It was not uncommon for people of this time to have two names. Saul is a Hebrew name and recalls King Saul of the Old Testament. Paul was a Greco-Roman name, which meant *small*. When Saul interacted primarily with the Jewish community, he used his Hebrew name. As he moved into ministry to the Gentiles, he began to use his Roman name. He is known as Paul for the remainder of Acts and throughout the letters he wrote.

When Paul set out for Paphos, he began the first of what would become three missionary journeys. The thirteen letters written by Paul and preserved in the New Testament were sent to churches Paul either visited on his mission trips or planned to visit.

Luke referred to two cities named Antioch. One was located just north of Palestine in Syria and was the place of the large Christian population. The second, part of Paul's missionary trip, was located north of the Mediterranean Sea in what is now south-central Turkey.

As was customary during these times, Paul was invited by the rulers of the local synagogue to preach to the people. In a fashion similar to Peter (2.29-31), Paul pointed to David, whose reign served as a climax after centuries of waiting through other types of leadership. Though David was a *man after My [God's] own heart,* he was not the long awaited Messiah. David had died, and his body had decayed or become corrupted. On the other hand, Jesus had suffered death at the hands of the rulers in Jerusalem because they did not know the words of the prophets. Unlike David, Jesus was raised from the dead, seen by multiple witnesses, and His body was not corrupted or decayed. All of this pointed to Jesus being the long awaited Messiah.

Justification is a term used to mean *made righteous before God*. The death of Jesus was payment for the sins of humanity in a way the Law of Moses never could be.

The Jewish leaders in the synagogue initially encouraged Paul and Barnabas, but later became jealous of the great following the men enjoyed. Their rejection was akin to judging themselves as unworthy of eternal life. Though the Jews rejected the message of Christ, the Gentiles rejoiced that they were included.

INSIGHTS

Paul and Barnabas set out on their first missionary journey because God spoke through the Holy Spirit to members of the Antioch church. Paul had already begun ministering to the Gentiles, and this served to confirm where God was calling Paul to serve. In a similar manner today, the Holy

Spirit can speak to another believer as a means of confirming for us the service God calls us to. Sometimes the call can seem much more difficult than anything we would envision for ourselves. The good news is that God never calls us to do something for which He does not also equip us. We can trust Him to provide what we need when we need it.

1. The church is seen consistently praying to God for guidance for their next step. Do you seek God consistently for direction in your life? In the lives of your family members? For the members of the Body of Christ to which you belong?

2. God's power over evil is displayed in His dealings with Elymas. What do you believe about God's ability to overcome evil? Is it evident in your daily dealings and attitudes toward life that Jesus defeated Satan on the cross?

3. Paul and Barnabas were filled with joy despite the persecution they endured. How do you respond to suffering and persecution? As a believer, are you able to experience deep joy knowing God's purpose and plan will be met, even if you can't see or don't understand what He is doing? Are you able to be joyful even if you are rejected because of Jesus?

Acts 14

BACKGROUND

Iconium was the capital of a region known as Lycaonia located in Asia Minor. It was approximately 120 miles north of the Mediterranean Sea and at the foot of the Tarsus mountains. Lystra and Derbe were cities in the same region. The region appears to have had its own language. It may have been a variation of Greek or it may have been completely different, requiring Paul and Barnabas to speak through interpreters.

OVERVIEW

City magistrates were given the authority to do whatever it took to end disturbances. One method of maintaining peace was to ban from the city those creating the disturbance. Since this was the case, the plot to kill Paul and Barnabas went beyond the law.

People sometimes thought those capable of working miracles were gods. A local legend told of the visit by Zeus and Hermes, ancient Greek gods. In the story, they received an indifferent reception because they were not recognized. Not wanting to make the same mistake, the local people not only welcomed Paul and Barnabas, but also treated them as gods.[6] Because of the language difference, it took Paul and Barnabas some time to understand what the people were saying. When they finally did, they tore their clothes—the Jewish response to blasphemy.

The sermon recorded here is a condensed version of the sermon Paul gave on the Areopagus (17.22-31). Because Paul was preaching to Gentiles who had no knowledge of the Hebrew scriptures, he focused

6 *New Bible Commentary: 21st Century Edition* (ed. D. A Carson et al.; Accordance electronic ed. Downers Grove: InterVarsity Press, 1994), 1087

on truths that were self-evident and led his listeners to Biblical truths.

Mobs often can change their behavior quickly, as happened with the people in Lystra. Not only did Paul and Barnabas deny they were gods, but they also denied the gods existed. Because they had worked miracles and denied they were gods, they became dangerous magicians in the eyes of the multitude.

The point of stoning was to kill the transgressor. Paul's survival and ability to walk afterwards points to divine protection upon him during the incident. Some have debated whether that protection was healing or resurrection. In either case, Paul lived and carried on his ministry.

Though Paul and Barnabas had suffered oppression in both Lystra and Iconium, they returned in order to strengthen the believers in those cities. They also ensured that each new church had elders who served as the church's leaders.

Paul and Barnabas returned to Antioch and the believers who had sent them out to report all that God had done in the midst of the Gentiles

INSIGHTS

Paul and Barnabas were able to speak with authority despite the opposition they faced. God's power does not manifest itself because of who is witnessing but as a result of what is being witnessed to. The same is true today. Our ability to speak with authority does not come from who we are as individuals but from the power of the truth we speak. In addition, God calls us to speak His truth but does not hold us responsible for how that truth is received. Each individual must make his or her own decision. Our responsibility is to share God's truth so others can make the right decision.

1. During Paul and Barnabas's travels to Iconium, they encountered many believers who encouraged them but also unbelieving Jews who were more interested in stirring up trouble than listening to the good news. In the face of this trial, Paul and Barnabas stayed considerably longer than planned. What is your first instinct when trouble arises? How often do you seek what God wants from you when it might be easier to flee the situation?

2. Paul and Barnabas were great supporters and encouragers to the young, growing church. How supportive are you towards the church and its leaders? Whom might you offer a word of encouragement to today?

Acts 15

BACKGROUND

In reference to direction, up and down tend to be viewed as referring to north and south today. In Old and New Testament times, however, it referred to elevation. Jerusalem was higher than the surrounding areas, so one traveled *up* to Jerusalem regardless of whether they were heading north or south.

OVERVIEW

Circumcision and adherence to the Law of Moses were the requirements for converting to Judaism. Some believed Christianity was a movement within Judaism and, therefore, required that one convert first to Judaism by being circumcised and then to Christianity. In this view, Jesus was a supplement to the Old Testament, rather than the long awaited Messiah and fulfillment of the Old Testament.

Paul and Barnabas, having witnessed God's movement in Gentiles who had not been circumcised, believed circumcision was an unnecessary burden and was not a sign of the New Covenant instituted by Christ. Ultimately, the question centered on what was required in order to experience salvation. If circumcision was required, then faith plus the law was needed. If salvation was the result of faith alone, then any additional requirements, including circumcision, were counterproductive.

Through his vision and experience with Cornelius, Peter had witnessed firsthand God's intent to include Gentiles. As a result, he supported Paul and Barnabas' contention that circumcision was not required.

This is the last mention of Peter in the book of Acts. His final statement is confirmation that salvation is experienced through faith in Christ and by His grace alone.

James was the half-brother of Jesus. Though he initially did not believe his brother was the Messiah, he later embraced the faith after the resurrected Jesus appeared to him (Jn. 7.5; 1 Cor. 15.7). He was also one of three men Paul described as pillars in the Jerusalem church (Gal. 2.9).

Although the testimony of Peter, Paul, and Barnabas was important to the council's decision, it was not all that was needed to make the decision. James looked to the Old Testament scriptures to find confirmation that God would indeed call the Gentiles to faith in Him (Amos 9.11-12).

James suggested four ways the Gentiles might change their lifestyle in order to live in harmony with the Jewish segment of the church. These four, namely, food offered to idols, sexual immorality, food from strangled animals, and meat with blood in it, were particularly offensive to the Jewish people.

In order to confirm the council's decision, a letter was written and carried back to the church in Antioch by trusted and recognized leaders from Jerusalem. Judas is a Hebrew name while Silas is a Hellenistic name. Though the text does not specifically state it, the names likely indicate that men from both sides of the debate were sent.

Unlike the efforts of the Jerusalem council to resolve the conflict over Gentile believers, Paul and Barnabas did not resolve their personal conflict over John Mark. This was not the same doctrinal issue as was presented to the council and the two decided to disagree while still fulfilling their call to preach God's word to the mission field.

INSIGHTS

Paul and Barnabas were able to discern between conflict that needed to be resolved and that on which they could agree to disagree. Today we often need to make the same distinction. Some conflicts have significant and lasting implications if we fail to come to a resolution. Other conflicts are less critical and failing to come to a resolution has a much smaller impact. Though the conflict was not initially resolved, later in his ministry, Paul sought out Mark's aid and companionship. Paul had not closed his heart to John Mark, just as we also should not close our hearts to those with whom we experience conflict.

1. Those who taught circumcision was still required brought sharp dispute among those being taught by Paul and Barnabas. As a result, Paul and Barnabas went to the apostles and elders in Jerusalem. Do you listen with a discerning ear when listening to claims about Jesus made by others? When you struggle with faith questions and the trials of life, how often do you seek out mature Christians for advice and counsel?

2. Early followers of Jesus struggled with what was required to be a believer. The Jews of the time, who didn't understand Jesus had come as the complete fulfillment of the law, demanded that the law, including circumcision, be maintained. Ultimately, those who understood Jesus' message of grace and redemption prevailed. Jesus' sacrificial death and subsequent resurrection mean believers are saved through grace alone. Nothing else is required. Do you believe this for yourself and others? What, if any, additional requirements are you consciously or subconsciously requiring of yourself or others in order to enjoy the gift of salvation God freely offers?

Acts 16

BACKGROUND

Public baths were common in New Testament times. As a result, it would have been much more evident who was circumcised and who was not than we experience today. A known Jew who was not circumcised would have had much less credibility with his fellow Jews than would a circumcised man.

A synagogue was formed in any city where ten Jewish male household heads could be found. If ten were not present in a city, a place of prayer, generally located near a river, was established.

OVERVIEW

Being obedient to the leading of the Holy Spirit, Paul traveled in a northwest direction across what is today Turkey. Once Paul reached Troas, all the places he visited were located on or near the coast of the Aegean Sea in what are modern-day Greece and Turkey.

For the first time in Acts, Luke uses the first person plural pronoun *we*. Because Luke was both meticulous and historically accurate in his writing, there is no reason to believe he meant anything other than that he accompanied Paul on this part of his missionary journey. This is the first of four such *we* sections in Acts (16.10-17; 20.5-15; 21.1-18; 27.1-28.16).

Purple dye was collected in small quantities from a certain type of mollusk. Because it was so laborious to collect, it was expensive and generally reserved for garments worn by royalty.

Some translations indicate Lydia traded the dye itself while others specify purple cloth. In either case, trade in such items likely meant she was a wealthy woman.

The original Greek states the slave girl had a *spirit of Python*. In Greek mythology, Apollo killed a serpent called Python and assumed his powers of prediction. A *spirit of Python* came to be known as a being controlled by an evil force. In this particular case, the girl does not appear to be insane or fraudulent but had the ability to earn money for her masters.

Though Paul and Silas had not preached anything that was against Roman law or customs, the slave girl's masters used this as a veiled way to get revenge for taking away their means of generating money.

Beating was a common means of securing evidence before a trial took place. It was also used as a means to humiliate the accused and discourage any followers. By law, Roman citizens were exempt from such treatment and were entitled to due process.

Roman guards were often executed if they allowed their prisoners to escape. Paul and Silas' reassurance prevented the guard from taking his own life and led to him putting his faith in Christ.

Under Roman custom, the members of a household would have followed whatever religious conventions the head of the household chose. Christianity, however, requires each person to make his/her own decision. As a result, Paul gave the *word of the Lord to him and to all who were in his house*.

By waiting until after he had been beaten to announce he was a Roman citizen, Paul put the magistrates in an awkward position. A complaint to higher authorities from Roman citizens who had been beaten and not given a fair trial put the magistrates at risk of losing their official positions.

Paul and Silas had been publicly beaten, giving many the impression they had done something wrong. Had they walked quietly away, they risked tainting the reputation of the fledgling church in Philippi by association.

INSIGHTS

It is interesting that just after resolving the issue of circumcision, Paul met a Jewish Christian whom he insisted be circumcised. Timothy, whose mother was Jewish and father was Greek, was a believer and his circumcision allowed him to be a credible witness to the Jewish community. His salvation was not in question as it had been for the Gentiles, so circumcision was acceptable. At times, we may find it necessary to identify with the people we witness to by adopting their customs. Such adaptations would never include anything immoral but could include things like dress and social conventions.

1. The Holy Spirit led Paul and Timothy to each place they visited. Do you invite the Holy Spirit to direct your steps? How much do you rely upon the Holy Spirit to direct what you do each day? In what ways could you intentionally seek more input from the Holy Spirit?

2. Paul and Silas's obedience to stay in prison after they were presented with an opportunity to escape led to the amazing story of salvation for the jailer and his family. When you are put into difficult situations, what motivates you more, seeking self-protection or looking for what God wants to do in the situation? In what way(s) might you take a step away from the security of seeking self-protection to be more open to what God might be planning to do through you?

Acts 17

BACKGROUND

Though Paul was repeatedly run out of cities in which he was witnessing, he did enough to establish a body of believers. He later wrote letters to encourage and admonish the believers in several of those cities/regions. First and Second Corinthians, Galatians, Ephesians, Philippians, Colossians, and 1 and 2 Thessalonians were written to the churches in Corinth, Galatia, Ephesus, Philippi, Colossae, and Thessalonica respectively.

OVERVIEW

When Paul *reasoned from the scriptures*, he pointed to Old Testament verses that prophesied the suffering, crucifixion, and resurrection of the Messiah and noted how accurately they foretold all Jesus had experienced.

Paul's accusers attempted to paint him as a revolutionary by referring to *King Jesus* and suggesting that this king would rule in Caesar's place. Such an attempted revolt led by zealous Jews took place in 49 A.D.

Taking security is similar to posting bond and was required of Jason to ensure there would be no repetition of the trouble and Paul would not return to Thessalonica.

Epicureans belonged to a group of philosophers who valued pleasure by avoiding physical pain and emotional disturbances. They also did not believe in God or viewed him as irrelevant and uninvolved. Stoics belonged to a school of philosophers who opposed the Epicureans because they believed pleasure should be avoided.[7]

The Greek term translated babbler referred to a bird picking up seed. It was later used as an insult and meant a worthless person.

The Areopagus was a council that had served a combined judicial and legislative function during Greek governance. By Paul's time, when Greece was part of the Roman Empire, the council functioned in more of an educational board/think tank role. It served to maintain the Athenian religion and could censor ideas but could not pass criminal judgment.[8] The council met on the Hill of Ares (Mars Hill in Latin).

Several centuries earlier, a disastrous plague had afflicted Athens. Prayers to the gods had no effect in combating the plague. It wasn't until a poet appealed to the unknown god that the horrible plague began to subside. An altar, still in existence during Paul's visit, commemorated the event.

Paul's gospel presentation began by pointing to a single God who created and controlled all things. Little in what Paul said would have been offensive to his listeners until he began to speak of the resurrected Christ. The Greek philosophers Socrates and Plato had taught that all physical things were evil and all spiritual things good. This idea had taken root in Greek thought making bodily resurrection a repulsive concept.

Though Paul's speech had little effect on his listeners, Dionysius, a prominent member of the Areopagus, as well as Damaris and others responded, creating enough of a base to begin a church in Athens. Other writers have named Dionysius as the first bishop of the church in Athens.[9]

INSIGHTS

The Bereans searched the scriptures to discover the truth of God's Word. These few verses hold great truth for us today. The world would have us

---

[7] Craig S. Keener, *The IVP Bible Background Commentary: New Testament* (Accordance electronic ed. Downers Grove: InterVarsity Press, 1993)

[8] *NIV Quest Study Bible*, (Grand Rapids, MI: Zondervan, 2003), 1591

[9] Earl Radmacher, Ronald B. Allen, and H. Wayne House, editors, *Nelson's New Illustrated Bible Commentary* (Nashville: Thomas Nelson Publishers)1403

believe the God of Christianity does not exist, we can each be our own god, and truth is relative to our own definition. We, too, can diligently search the scriptures to determine whether what we hear aligns with God's truth—the only truth. Anything that is not confirmed by His truth should be rejected, and that which is confirmed can be wholeheartedly embraced. Care must be taken, however, to interpret the scriptures as the writers/God intended, not to suit our own purposes.

1. As Paul continued his missionary travels, he encountered the Bereans who received Paul's message with eagerness and examined the scriptures daily to ensure what they were hearing was actually true. How often do you take what you hear at face value? Do you eagerly read God's word each day, especially to ensure you recognize both the truth and the lies of those around you?

2. When Paul arrived in Athens, he was not afraid of the different habits and culture he encountered there. How do you respond to people from other cultures? Paul was able to share the truth by referring to an idea within the culture all the people could relate to. Do you seek to find common ground when talking to people from different cultures?

Acts 18

BACKGROUND

Corinth was the capital of Achaia, a region that encompassed most of modern day Greece. It served as a rival to Athens. It hosted a variety of religions including a worship center for Aphrodite (the goddess of fertility) and an important temple for Apollo.

Alexandria, a seaport on the northern coast of Egypt, was the second largest city in the Roman Empire. The Hebrew scriptures were translated into Greek in Alexandria about one hundred fifty years before the birth of Jesus. Today we know this translation at the Septuagint.

OVERVIEW

Depending on the region in which one learned his trade, a tentmaker could be someone who worked with leather or cloth. Cilicia, the region from which Paul came, was noted for its felted cloth made from goat hair. It is likely that Paul was involved in making such cloth or in using the cloth to make tents. In this manner, Paul was able to support himself in cities where no churches yet existed.

Unlike today when people making the same product function as competitors, in Paul's time, people making the same product often banded together, formed guilds, and worked side by side.

Paul maintained his habit of going to the synagogues first to proclaim Jesus to the Jews. Experiencing little success, Paul turned his focus to the Gentiles.

Paul had experienced some harsh treatment in other locations where he proclaimed the gospel message. God encouraged Paul to speak boldly as he would not suffer harsh treatment in Corinth.

Evidence of God's promise became apparent when charges were once again leveled against Paul. This time, he did not have to defend himself. The proconsul, having already been apprised of the events, determined that what Paul was preaching was a sect of Judaism and not an illegal new religion or in any other manner in violation of Roman law.

Though the text does not state the specific reason Paul had his hair cut, it was likely done in conjunction with a Nazarite vow (Num. 6) he had made. Such vows were generally made in gratitude for God's blessing or as petition for future blessings. Paul may have been thanking God for his safekeeping in Corinth. Such vows were to be fulfilled in Jerusalem, hence Paul's journey home.

John's baptism was the baptism John the Baptist advocated in preparation for the coming of the Messiah. John's disciples had scattered into Asia Minor and Egypt and evidently had not heard about Jesus' death and resurrection.

Pricilla and Aquila, who had learned about the truth of Jesus from Paul, now became teachers of the truth as they shared the good news with Apollo. Apollo then traveled to Corinth to encourage the believers there.

INSIGHTS

Paul trusted God to do as He promised and so spoke boldly in Corinth. When he left the city unharmed, he showed his gratitude by making a Nazarite vow. Though Christians do not make Nazarite vows, we can still follow the pattern Paul set. First, we must trust God as He sends us to speak His Word to people who need to hear the truth of the Risen Christ. Then, we can show our gratitude. We may not receive the same promise of safety God gave Paul, but we will experience His blessings as we are obedient to His will.

1. Paul was greatly encouraged when the Lord spoke to him about his mission. How do you hear God speak to you? Do you listen for His confirmation and encouragement on your life journey?

2. Paul did not pass up the opportunity to strengthen the disciples as he traveled through Galatia and Phrygia. How well do you see the opportunities God's presents to you to strengthen both friends and strangers as you go about your daily activities? Do you freely spend time with those needing encouragement without asking for anything in return?

Acts 19

BACKGROUND

Asia was a province in the Roman Empire and should not be confused with the larger region known as Asia Minor.

The term translated *book* likely refers to small pieces of papyri rolled up and placed either in cylinders or lockets worn around the neck. The papyri contained magical incantations and were so popular in Ephesus that they became known as Ephesian writings in other Greco-Roman literature.

OVERVIEW

The disciples, or students, of John the Baptist must have lacked a measure of inspiration that was evident to Paul when he encountered them. With full knowledge of Jesus' truth and receipt of the Holy Spirit, the men of Ephesus expressed the same power of the Spirit as the apostles had on Pentecost.

Laying on of hands was not necessary to receive the Holy Spirit (10.44-48). By doing so here, Paul demonstrated his authority as an apostle and affirmed the unity of the church in Ephesus with the body of believers in Jerusalem.

Paul preached for three months, but when it became evident that the Jews were not receiving the message, Paul withdrew with his disciples. Tyrannus was likely the name of a philosopher who had a room or building in which Paul and his disciples could meet. Because all in Asia heard about Jesus, Paul and his students were doing more than just studying Jesus' teachings. Paul must have been sending students out in much the same manner Jesus had sent His own disciples out.

Handkerchiefs and aprons were used in Paul's trade. One was tied around the head to soak up perspiration, the other around the waist to protect clothing. Why God would use these items to perform miracles is unclear. Some have speculated that since Ephesus was a center for magicians, wizards, and wandering priests, God perhaps used such unusual means to demonstrate His superior power.

According to ancient tradition, exorcists could coax an evil spirit out of a person by invoking the name of the deity or spirit. Since the power of Jesus' name was widespread by this time, it is likely that these exorcists, who did not believe in Jesus, attempted to exploit the heavenly power by invoking Jesus' name. They quickly learned that this power is not available for the taking but comes only through knowing Jesus personally.

Recognizing that Paul's Jesus could not be manipulated like other spirits, many came to believe. Magicians brought their books of spells, formulas, and astrological forecasts to burn them publicly as a testimony to their new beliefs. The total price for that which was burned was roughly equivalent to an average worker's wages for one hundred thirty-six years.

Some versions translate the temple goddess' name as Diana, while others use Artemis. Small shrines with miniature images of this goddess of fertility could be found throughout the city.

Seeing the large number of converts to the new religion, Demetrius and his fellow silversmiths felt their livelihood threatened. As a result, money motivated the attempted attack against Paul.

INSIGHTS

Just as the magicians and exorcists tried to take advantage of the power they perceived to be behind the name of Jesus, so unscrupulous people try to do the same today. The underlying interest of some faith healers, prayer cloth peddlers, and prosperity gospel preachers is in the profit they can make by convincing people they speak in the name of Jesus.

Falling for their schemes rarely produces the desired results, while the preachers often seem to enjoy great wealth and pleasure. God never promised our walk with Him would be easy and trouble-free. He did promise to walk with us all the days of our lives.

1. The people of Ephesus had a limited understanding of Christ, yet their hearts received the truth John had planted. The Spirit was quick to respond to their desire to know and live the truth of Christ. Where is your heart in relation to receiving Christ's truth? Are you open to the Holy Spirit's direction and leading?

2. Paul traveled throughout the Roman Empire because he was confident of God's call on his life to spread the gospel message. Do you know God has called each of us to spread the gospel throughout our spheres of influence? What can you do in your arena to help ensure Christ's good news is available to anyone who wants to hear it?

Acts 20

BACKGROUND

Though not clear from Acts, the purpose of this trip was to collect offerings from several of the new churches (Philippi, Thessalonica, and Corinth) for the believers in Jerusalem. Paul made references to collecting these offerings in several of his letters (Rom. 15.26; 1 Cor. 16.1-4).

OVERVIEW

It appears that Paul left Luke in Philippi. Once he returned, Luke rejoined him and the *we* of the text resumed.

The Greek word translated *encourage* has a range of meanings, including instruction, appeal, affirmation, warning, and correction.

The Jewish Sabbath was celebrated from Friday evening through Saturday evening. Christians started meeting on Sunday, the first day of the week, in commemoration of the Resurrection, which occurred on Sunday (Luke 24.1; John 20.1).

Paul and his companions briefly parted ways in Troas. The companions took a ship to Assos while Paul made the journey on foot. Why Paul felt a need to do this is unknown. Some speculate Paul needed time on his own to pray and seek guidance from God. Whatever the reason, once he arrived in Assos, he was in a hurry to get to Jerusalem with the offerings he and his companions had collected.

Ancient historians tended to write speeches they were recording in their own words, often because there was no word-for-word record of such speeches or because writers often heard about them from a third party. It is interesting to note that the recording of this speech is more in Paul's style than in Luke's, pointing to direct contact between the two.

With the leaders of the church in Ephesus gathered, Paul delivered a farewell speech. He hinted at the coming trials and imprisonment he would shortly endure and encouraged the leaders to be strong as they faced their own coming trials.

Paul's claim to be innocent of all men's blood was a reference to Old Testament scriptures that made one responsible for the death of a wicked man if the opportunity to speak truth was passed up (Ezek. 3.18-19; 33.8-9). Paul claimed he had held nothing back and had spoken the message of Christ at every opportunity.

Luke recorded a quote of Jesus' not found in the gospels.

Paul's final visit with the elders of the church of Ephesus took place approximately 56 A.D., about 25 years after Jesus' resurrection. By that time, numerous oral and written traditions would have been circulating. The gospel writers did not record everything Jesus did and spoke (John 21.25). Therefore, this was a statement Paul heard from another source.

INSIGHTS

It is evident that great affection existed between Paul and the elders from Ephesus. The sorrow of the elders came not only from the knowledge that they would not see Paul again, but also that they would not hear him speak. Paul spoke the good news of Jesus Christ, giving the elders and all believers in Ephesus the opportunity to experience the freedom of the gospel message. While Paul's personality may have provided some attraction in the relationship between Paul and the church, it was ultimately the truth and hope Paul spoke that provided the greatest attraction.

1. Paul was headed to Jerusalem even though the Holy Spirit had warned him that prison and hardship were waiting. How dedicated are you to serving God with all that you are? If you were certain of fulfilling God's will and plan for you, would you willingly go into a dangerous situation? Do you agree or disagree with the following statement: It is better to be in a dangerous place in God's will than a safe place out of God's will? Why did you answer the way you did?

2. Paul warned the elders that people will rise up to distract and distort the message of Christ. Are you on guard for those around you who do the same? Are you spending enough time reading and studying scripture to be able to recognize when the message you are hearing is filled with lies and mistruths?

ACTS 21

BACKGROUND

Some Gentile Christians believe Jewish Christians (today called Messianic Jews) need to cease practicing customs that are a significant part of their cultural and national heritage. As God's called people, Jews complete their faith by believing Christ to be the long promised Messiah. Jews are free to continue their cultural practices while Gentiles are not called to assimilate such practices. Unity within the Body of Christ while respecting the practices of other cultures is of the highest importance.

OVERVIEW

Paul wanted to be in Jerusalem for Pentecost. Since he had celebrated Passover in Philippi three weeks earlier, he had approximately thirty days to get from Miletus to Jerusalem.

Paul had been bound or compelled by the Spirit to go to Jerusalem (20.22). The disciples urged Paul *through the Spirit* not to go to Jerusalem. Since the Spirit had already directed Paul to go, this more likely signified the danger Paul would be in when he arrived in Jerusalem, rather than a warning not to go. For the disciples, Paul was a beloved and highly respected brother in Christ and they did not want to see him hurt.

The prophesying of Philip's four virgin daughters was fulfillment of the Joel prophecy Peter quoted after the coming of the Holy Spirit on Pentecost (2.16-17; Joel 2.28-32).

Agabus appeared earlier in Acts to make a prophecy about the future (11.27-28). Here he predicted the imprisonment and suffering

Paul would face when he went to Jerusalem. Agabus did not warn Paul not to go to Jerusalem, he just expressed the opposition Paul would face when he went.

Receiving Paul and his companions *gladly* or *warmly* would have included normal Jewish hospitality: lodging in Jewish-Christian homes for all in the party (including any uncircumcised Gentiles), meals, and meeting any reasonable needs.

Concern was expressed that Paul was teaching Jewish believers they should no longer observe the Law of Moses. In fact, Paul himself was observing the Law. His reason for returning to Jerusalem was to worship as prescribed by the Law. Paul adamantly opposed the belief of some that Gentiles believers needed to become *Jewish* in order to become Christian also. James suggested Paul join four men who were completing the requirements of Nazirite vow they had taken as a show of Paul's support for the Jewish law.

Extra-biblical texts from this time indicate that Jewish nationalism was on the rise. Increasingly less tolerance was shown for any deviations from the observation of strict Judaism.

The garrison was the Fortress Antonia located on the northwest side of the temple. Between six hundred and one thousand troops were stationed there and they needed only to walk through a tunnel to enter the outer court.

The commander wrongly assumed Paul could not speak Greek because he was the Egyptian Jew who had caused trouble earlier. Likely thinking the crowd had made the same error, the commander allowed Paul to speak to the crowd.

INSIGHTS

Though Paul's friends had repeatedly been warned of what was in store for Paul when he entered Jerusalem, they continued their journey with him. The remainder of Paul's life would be marked by a variety of friends who stood by him during some intense trials. Not all of us are Pauls who traverse the world sharing the good news of Christ, but all of us benefit from sincere and devoted relationships with good friends. Friendships of this sort occur because we are intentional about developing such relationships, not because we wait passively for someone else to approach us.

1. Paul was so certain that the Holy Spirit was leading him to Jerusalem that he was willing to forgo the warnings shared with him by people he knew and trusted. When God has given you a mission, is there a time to heed the warnings of others? Do you try to dissuade people going to dangerous places to do God's work, especially when the people are confident of God's calling on their lives?

2. Although Paul was set on going to Jerusalem, he was also willing to follow the advice of those who wished to minimize the risk he was taking. Where is your heart in relation to the input of others? When others, especially family members, are clearly following the Lord, are you able to release them and give them your blessing, even if you would prefer they did not leave?

Acts 22

BACKGROUND

Several means existed by which one could become a Roman citizen. The most common was to be born to a Roman father (as Paul was). Others included being the citizen of a Roman colony; retiring from auxiliary military duty; being part of a group that was granted citizenship by Rome; being a freed slave of a Roman owner. Purchasing a Roman citizenship was not common. It generally occurred when a slave bought his/her freedom or if one found an official who would accept a bribe.

OVERVIEW

Paul's defense before the crowd was the first of five he would make.

This is the second of three accounts of Paul's encounter with the risen Christ. Though Paul was quite aware of his Jewish heritage and that of his audience, he was also unwilling to compromise his calling to the Gentile people.

Gamaliel was a student of the renowned Hillel and himself a well-known teacher of the law whose name would likely have been recognized by some in the crowd.

Paul tried to identify with the crowd by stating that he too had been zealous for God in a manner similar to that being exhibited by the crowd.

The crowd's reaction to Paul's mention of the Gentiles was predictable. With Jewish nationalism on the rise, the people were not inclined in any manner to associate with those who were not Jewish.

Paul had experienced several beatings with scourges prior to the one he faced here. Those performed by the Roman military were done with leather straps onto which were fastened small pieces of metal and were much worse than anything Paul had previously experienced. Scourging often resulted in permanent scarring, maiming, or even death. Roman citizens were exempt from torture for the purposes of gathering information. They also were entitled to due process of the law before any type of punishment was inflicted.

As in his earlier experience, Paul waited until the law had been violated to reveal his Roman citizenship in order to gain the legal upper hand.

INSIGHTS

Twice, Paul waited shrewdly until he had received some sort of ill treatment before revealing his Roman citizenship. This afforded him some legal maneuvering room. Though not illegal, Paul's shrewdness is reminiscent of the parable Jesus told about the unjust servant (Luke 16.1-8). We too can use shrewdness to do God's will. It may involve withholding information as Paul did or take a variety of other forms. What is important is that such shrewdness does not involve illegal activity, is honoring to God, and serves to advance God's kingdom rather than our own interests.

1. Paul's conversion story illustrates how God was able to use both Paul's training in the law and persecution of Christians to bring glory to Himself. Even though Paul's prior life was filled with sin against God, God used Paul in mighty ways for His kingdom. How do you view your past? Do you trust God to use your life, sins and all, for His purposes and to further His kingdom? Have you sought God's forgiveness by confessing your sins?

2. Paul was very strategic about the timing of revealing his Roman citizenship. Are you able to be strategic in your interactions with those who oppose you? How well do you rely on God to provide you with what needs to be said when it needs to be said (Matt. 10.16-20)?

Acts 23

BACKGROUND

The events recorded here occurred approximately 58 A.D., when Ananias was high priest for the second time (47-52 and about 53-59). Ananias was known for his greed and for stealing the tithes that belonged to poorer priests. As high priest, he was serving as a Roman vassal. Jewish Zealot revolutionaries eventually killed Ananias in 66 A.D.

Jerusalem served as the location of the Jewish government while Caesarea housed the Roman government for the region.

OVERVIEW

The law outlined a procedure for settling a dispute between two parties. Only when the wicked party was identified was s/he to be beaten, not before. Paul was defending himself and no judgment had been pronounced. Therefore, Ananias' order to strike Paul was against the law (Deut. 25.1-3). Though Ananias did not actually strike Paul, he deserved the rebuke because he had ordered the action.

Whitewash was a thin coating of white paint used to make dirty things appear clean. The structure had not been changed, only the appearance.

Normally, the high priest was dressed in distinctive robes and sat in a special place. It has been suggested that Paul did not recognize the high priest because, in this special session of the Sanhedrin, the high priest was not dressed or seated as he normally would have been. The high priest had changed a number of times in the twenty years that had passed since Paul had regular contact with the Sanhedrin and he may not have known who the current high priest was.

While the Pharisees believed in the resurrection of the dead, the Sadducees did not. Paul, a Pharisee himself, appealed to the belief in life after death. Paul had not only taught about the resurrection but that Jesus was the fulfillment of that same resurrection the Pharisees believed to be true. Upon understanding that the accusation against Paul centered on this teaching, the Pharisees called for his release.

Once again, God reassured Paul that he was right where he was supposed to be. Not only would he have an opportunity to testify to God's glory in Jerusalem, but in Rome as well.

The weakness of the council's case against Paul was evident by their willingness to participate in an assassination plot. Had they had a strong case, the law would have brought about the outcome they desired.

A large contingent of soldiers was sent with Paul to protect him. Palestine was experiencing a period of great unrest and attacks at night by robbers were not uncommon. A large contingent was necessary for safe passage, especially at night.

Caesarea is approximately 60 miles north of Jerusalem. Antipatris was about thirty-five miles north and downhill of Jerusalem. To complete this distance overnight would have required a faster pace than most travelers journeyed at. The remainder of the journey to Caesarea was through open plains. Since ambush was much less likely there, the foot soldiers were sent back to Jerusalem.

The commander's letter was required for all prisoners sent to their superiors for examination. It was written in the standard form of the times.

INSIGHTS

For Paul, the prison ordeal was one that would last for several years and, tradition holds, finally result in his death. Though the church fervently prayed for Paul's release, God determined that the witness Paul would provide during this extended imprisonment would best serve His glory.

Likewise, many of us suffer through great and extended trials. God has determined that the witness we have in such circumstances will best serve His purposes. Although they are difficult and cause great anguish, we, like Paul, can gain comfort from knowing that God's purposes are being served in ways that would otherwise be impossible.

1. Paul was able to state that he had fulfilled his duty to God in good conscience because he had singularly dedicated himself to following Jesus from the time of his conversion until he spoke those words. If you were to stand before God today could you say the same? Remembering Paul did not start out his life as a Christ follower, what changes might you need to make in the way you live out your faith in order to say the same at the end of your life?

2. Paul was not alone when he spent the night in the barracks. We are told the Lord stood near and spoke a message of encouragement to Paul. When have you sensed the Lord standing near to you? How have you heard Him speaking words of encouragement to you?

Acts 24

BACKGROUND

Felix ruled Judea from 52 to 60 A.D. He had been a slave but had been able to gain his freedom. His brother was a friend of Claudius, the emperor, and was able to secure him a promising political career. Felix was not popular with his peers, was reported as very corrupt (he was said to have a king's power and a slave's character by a Roman historian), and regularly pursued all kinds of lustful desires.

OVERVIEW

Legal manuals of the time emphasized winning the judge's favor. Both the prosecution and Paul started off by praising Felix.

Three charges were brought against Paul: political treason (creating dissension or riots among the Jews throughout the world), religious heresy (leader of the Nazarene sect), and temple desecration (attempted only, since no witnesses had seen a foreigner actually enter the temple).

Being called a Nazarene was likely an insult to begin with. It was derived from the obscurity of Jesus' hometown. In time, Jewish Christians applied it to themselves.

Paul initially pointed to the ridiculousness of the political treason charge. He had been in the country for only twelve days, hardly enough time to incite riots. He also contended that although he was a follower of the Way, he believed in the Law and the Prophets. He was, therefore, a follower of Judaism, a recognized religion of the Roman Empire.

Drusilla, originally married to the king of Syria, divorced her husband at Felix's instigation and became his third wife (he had divorced his previous wives). Drusilla was the great-granddaughter of Herod the Great (who tried to have Jesus killed), the great niece of Herod Antipas (who beheaded John the Baptist), and daughter of Herod Agrippa (who had James put to death). Drusilla's Jewish heritage likely played a role in the time Felix spent listening to Paul.

Paul shared with Felix the good news of Christ, but it is likely that when Paul began talking about righteousness, self-control, and the judgment to come that Felix was convicted of his own guilt and refused to listen to anything further Paul had to say.

Felix had hoped the Gentiles would provide bribe money to secure Paul's release, and this was no doubt part of Felix's motivation to talk to Paul. Paul, on the other hand, was interested only in sharing the life-saving news of Christ.

Porcius Festus succeeded Felix as governor after Felix crushed a riot with more force than was actually necessary. Felix may have wanted *to do the Jews a favor* because he needed all the mercy and political support he could muster.

INSIGHTS

Despite his circumstances, Paul remained focused on his calling—sharing the good news of Christ. We should remember this attitude when we find ourselves in prolonged trials. God promises to use all things to bring about good in the lives of those who believe in Christ (Rom. 8.28). In the middle of such protracted circumstances, it is often hard, even impossible, to see how God could possibly bring anything good out of what we experience. It may even be that we won't know until we experience the glory of heaven. Nevertheless, we can trust that God *always* keeps His promises and our suffering will not be in vain.

1. God protected Paul through this violent time because He was still using Paul for His Kingdom purposes. Are there any forces that can thwart God's will and purposes from coming to pass? How would you rank your confidence that, despite the evil and corruption we see in the world today, God will ultimately triumph? If your confidence is not very strong, are you willing to pray that God would show you how to have more confidence in Him?

2. Paul was so focused on his goal to share Christ with anyone who would listen he was even willing to share the good news of Christ with the man who would be his judge. Are you this razor focused when it comes to sharing the gospel? How often do you pray God would give you opportunities to speak His truth to those who need to hear it?

ACTS 25

BACKGROUND

Historians portrayed Festus much more positively than they did Felix. Festus appears to have dealt with disturbances less harshly and caught many of those leading revolts.

Agrippa II was the son of Herod Agrippa I, king of Judea. He was a descendant of Herod the Great and the last of the Herodian dynasty. He was too young to assume the throne when his father died so was given a smaller territory in northern Judea to govern. He retained the right to appoint the high priest and was considered an expert in Jewish law.

OVERVIEW

Once again, the Jewish authorities tried to deal with Paul by planning an ambush while he was transported.

Sitting on the judgment seat, also translated as *convening the court,* meant Festus was holding an official hearing.

Festus had a reputation for being a more accommodating and fairer governor than Judea had experienced in the past. This likely provided Festus' motivation to *do the Jews a favor.*

A governor did not have to have full knowledge of the law. He generally had a council who was well versed in it and served as a resource when needed. The governor was not bound by the advice of the counsel, however.

By law, Roman citizens had the right to appeal for a trial before the Roman judgment seat, rather than the local authorities. The emperors generally delegated the hearing and judgment to others. It was less common for a Roman citizen to request the appeal before judgment had been handed down, but not unheard of. In this case, Paul was likely convinced he would not receive a fair trial before the Jewish Sanhedrin. The appeal was beneficial to Felix; it freed him from making the judgment as well as from dealing with the disappointed Jewish leadership if his judgment was different from what they were seeking.

Bernice was Agrippa's sister. Some historians claimed there was an incestuous relationship between the two while others vehemently denied it.

The charge against Paul was political, but all the evidence provided was religious in nature. Roman authorities were not normally well versed in Jewish law, so Paul's case left them at a loss as to how to judge it. Agrippa was the first who was well versed in both and could offer Festus an evaluation for his letter to the emperor.

INSIGHTS

God has set all rulers in their place to further His kingdom (Dan. 2.21, Rom13.1). Paul's appeal to Caesar was not placing trust in Caesar but trusting that God would work through the rulers He had set in place. God the Father used Roman soldiers to scourge His Son and later used Roman soldiers to transport Paul and keep him safe. Just as Paul exercised his rights as a Roman citizen so we too should understand we are endowed by our *Creator with certain unalienable Rights* and when appropriate, use the rights outlined in the US Constitution in our defense.

1. As a Roman citizen, Paul knew both the value of his citizenship and his right to appeal to Caesar. How much do you value your heavenly citizenship? Do you know your "rights" as a citizen of heaven? Those rights include calling God our Father, living in the value and worth in which we were created, and exercising the power God gives us to extend and receive forgiveness. Are there areas in which you have allowed the world to trample on your heavenly right or places in which you need to reclaim the power and freedom your rights give you?

2. All of the pomp and circumstances of the investigation and trial led to the fulfillment of Christ's words to Paul in Acts 23:11 that he would go to Rome. God's promises are always realized. Do you take God at His word? Do you believe in God's sovereignty over the world? In the midst of trying circumstances, are you able to rest in God's peace and promises to you as Paul was?

Acts 26

BACKGROUND

Roman citizens were afforded certain benefits in the empire that were denied to foreigners living within its boundaries and under its laws. One such benefit was the right to appeal a case to the emperor. Though lower courts were given an extensive range under which they could make judgments, it appears that once an appeal to the emperor had been made, it could not be revoked.

OVERVIEW

Paul's history as a Pharisee was important to his defense. He made it clear he was not starting a new religion but was a Jew who was living out his faith to a greater degree than most.

While God had promised many things to the Jewish people, the two most anticipated promises were the resurrection of the righteous and the simultaneous re-establishment of the twelve tribes.

In ancient trials, probability was given greater weight than hard evidence obtained from witnesses. As a result, Paul had to counter the supposition that the resurrection was improbable. He did so by reminding his listeners of God's great power and that the resurrection was a part of the most fundamental of Jewish hopes.

After relating his experience on the road to Damascus, Paul began to present evidence that the truths he spoke were congruent with the Old Testament. This was important because new religions were not permitted in the Roman Empire. By showing he was part of an existing, recognized, and condoned ethnic religion in the Roman Empire, Paul avoided the judgment associated with starting a new religion.

As Agrippa and Paul continued their dialogue, Agrippa realized Paul had gone beyond presenting evidence and was trying to convince him of the truth Paul taught. Had Agrippa denied belief in the prophets, he would have angered the Jews. Had he acknowledged belief in the prophets, he would have provided credibility to Paul's words. In an effort to sidestep the issue and appear to remain neutral, Agrippa ended the conversation.

INSIGHTS

In Paul's unique encounter with the risen Lord Jesus, he learned the truth, placed his faith in Christ, and experienced the grace of forgiveness of sins. Paul did not stop there, however. His experience became the basis for his obedience to the call God had given him to minister to the Gentiles. In a similar manner, as we have our own encounters with the risen Christ, come to faith, and experience His grace, we should not stop there, either. God calls each of us to participate in the fulfillment of His plan on earth. Our obedience to that call is not only important but will also prove to be the most satisfying of all we can do with our lives.

1. Paul stated that he had not been disobedient to the vision Jesus had given during their encounter when Paul was traveling to Damascus. How obedient are you to the commands God gives you? If your level of obedience needs improving, what might you do to gain confidence in God and knowing that whatever He asks comes out of His love for you and all people?

2. When Paul appeared before both Festus and King Agrippa, he was, as Peter would write a short time later, ready to give a defense to everyone who asked for the reason for the hope that was in him (1 Peter 3.15). Would you be able to give a defense for the hope that lies within you? If you are not, what one step can you take today that would begin preparing you to give the answer?

Acts 27

BACKGROUND

Summer winds generally blew from the west or northwest across the Mediterranean, making travel to the west slow and arduous. Crete could serve as a wind block when the conditions became particularly hazardous. There were several harbors along its southern shore. The southern shore began slanting in a northwesterly direction past the port of Fair Havens. Phoenix, located on this more exposed portion of the island, could be less protected and difficult to sail into depending on the direction and strength of the winds.

OVERVIEW

Luke resumes a we narrative, indicating that he accompanied Paul on the journey.

Some translations state Julius was a member of the Augustan Regiment, while others state it was the Imperial Regiment. This may have been an honorary title or a special unit in the military that was responsible for escorting prisoners or items such as food supplies to Rome and performing other special duties.

The *other prisoners* may have been other Roman citizens who had requested their case be heard by the emperor, but more likely they were convicted criminals under a death sentence being sent to Rome to appear as combatants in games for entertainment.

The *Fast* referred to the Day of Atonement, which occurred in September or October. The winds at this time of year made travel by sea very dangerous.

The favorable wind that would have gotten the ship to Phoenix in a few hours quickly changed direction and became a dangerous northern wind. Some translations use the more technical terms *tempestuous, Euraquilo,* and *Euroclydon* to describe the winds. Tempestuous is the root of *typhoon*, while *Euroclydon* or *Euraquilo* was the name given to storms coming out of the northeast.

The skiff or lifeboat was a small boat used to assist with mooring or tacking. It was often towed behind the ship and could be carried on deck when necessary.

Because ships could come apart in storms, one method of strengthening the ship was to run cables or ropes around the width of the ship to hold it together. The cables or ropes would likely have been dropped from either side of the bow and worked back along the sides of the ship before being secured.

Jettisoning the cargo would have been a normal step when faced with severe conditions. In the worst of weather, it would have taken all the manpower on board to lower the ship's tackle (rigging lines, booms, and spar). Whenever possible, these would have been secured to the ship for later use, but in the most severe conditions, they were thrown overboard so as not to further burden the ship.

The Adriatic Sea in ancient times encompassed a much larger area than it does today. Some have suggested that the term is actually *Adrian* or *Hadrian*, the name used for the central portion of the Mediterranean Sea between Greece, Italy, and Africa.

Alexandrian grain ships were reported to carry as many as six hundred people.

Guards were responsible for their prisoners but were less liable if a prisoner died at sea rather than escaped.

INSIGHTS

God had previously told Paul he would testify in Rome. He did not, however, state how Paul would get to Rome. Although Paul could be confident of eventually getting to Rome, the journey proved full of hazards and, more importantly, opportunities to testify to the goodness of God. Likewise, we may receive a word or calling from God regarding a particular destination, but our focus cannot be so completely on arriving that we miss the opportunities God presents on the journey. God has a purpose for us at the destination, but that does not eliminate additional purposes along the way.

1. Paul warned the sailors not to set sail, yet they went anyway and experienced the disaster Paul predicted. Do you have trusted Christian friends or mentors to whom you have given permission to speak into your life? How well do you listen when others warn that you are headed toward disaster? How do you discern between those who are acting as God's mouthpiece and those who are speaking out of their own values and desires?

2. God told Paul that all the men would survive the shipwreck despite not listening to Paul's advice. Can you think of a time when God has protected you despite not listening to His warnings? Have you expressed your gratitude to God for His ongoing protection and provision for your needs? If you have not, take a few minutes to do so now.

Acts 28

BACKGROUND

Italy relied quite heavily on Egypt for grain and as much as 150,000 tons of grain may have been shipped each year. Ships as long as 180 feet were built to transport the grain and were known as the Alexandrian fleet. It was the largest mercantile fleet in Europe prior to the 1700s.

OVERVIEW

Malta was on the shipping route between Rome and Egypt. Though descendants of the Phoenicians inhabited it, Roman citizens and retired soldiers had also settled on the island.

The justice the islanders expected to come to Paul after the snake bit may have referred to the goddess *Justice* who carried out the will of Fortune or Fates.

A fever common to Malta, Gibraltar, and other Mediterranean islands was traced in more modern times to a microorganism in goats' milk.[10] Some believe Publius's father was sick with this fever, though others contend the fever did not appear until well after Paul's time.

The Twin Brothers or Castor and Pollux were the twin sons of Zeus, whom sailors revered as protectors.

Puteoli was a port for the Alexandrian grain fleet and, as a result, many cultures including Jewish could all be found in the city. Christians had already been to Italy to share the good news of Christ and a community of believers could be found in Rome as well as other regions

[10] Earl Radmacher, Ronald B. Allen, and H. Wayne House, editors, *Nelson's New Illustrated Bible Commentary* (Nashville: Thomas Nelson Publishers) 1418

of Italy. Paul's letter to the Romans had been written approximately two years prior to his arrival.

The Christians who greeted Paul so enthusiastically offered hospitality not only to Paul but his captors as well, which was graciously accepted.

Settlements often developed around isolated inns and retained the name of the inn. Three Inns was located thirty-three Roman miles from Rome along the Appian Way, a heavily traveled, paved road.

Paul had not been accused of a serious crime, so may have been permitted to dwell in a house under house arrest. This would have allowed him to see visitors and entertain guests freely.

The leaders of the Jews were the leaders of the various synagogues in the region. Each synagogue in Rome functioned somewhat autonomously as there was no Jewish governing body in Rome. As Paul spoke to the leaders, he emphasized, as he had in the past, the continuity between the Old Testament and the life of Christ.

Little evidence exists that suggests that the Jewish community was universally hostile to Christians, though its skepticism was natural. Paul quoted Isaiah (6.9-10) to show that God's chosen people had fulfilled the ancient prophecy by rejecting God's message.

It is likely that Luke recorded events up to the then present moment and sent the letter off to its intended recipient. Since Acts was not written as a biography of Paul, this would account for the abrupt end.

Tradition holds that Paul was released after two years (according to Roman law), ministered in Spain as he had desired (Rom. 15.24), was eventually rearrested, retried, found guilty, and executed in Rome as a martyr between 64-67 A.D.

INSIGHTS

Except for approximately 220 years when Malta fell under Arab occupation, the island has been Christian since the time of Paul's shipwreck. Paul likely would never have imagined that his visit of three months would lead to thousands of years of faith in Christ. We, too, can have as lasting an impact as Paul did. God has called His people to spread His Word. When we are obedient to the direction and leading of the Holy Spirit, the impact of His Word can go far beyond what we imagine.

1. Even under house arrest, Paul found an audience who needed to hear the gospel message. Do you look for an opportunity in every circumstance to tell others about Christ? When all seems to be lost, does your faith in God remain strong enough to share the good news with those who need to hear? If not, how might God be calling you to trust Him more fully?

2. Paul was protected from the snakebite because God's plan was not yet complete. How have you seen God protect you so that you can complete all He has planned for you?

Acknowledgements

There are an amazing number of people who are involved in a project like this. First, my thanks go to Dave Wood for asking me to write a series of New and Old Testament notes to accompany our church's Bible reading program. Dave saw something in me that I did not see. As a result, I had the privilege and blessing of seeing God's hand work in and through me in most unexpected ways.

Thanks also go to the leadership and staff of Grace Community Church, in particular our previous pastor Bryan Hochhalter, current pastor Doug Kempton, Bryce Gray, Paula Smith, Tracey Krusz, and others who worked behind the scenes.

Thank you to Eddie Jones and Lighthouse Publishing of the Carolinas. Eddie's vision for my manuscript and belief in what I had written has been an enormous encouragement and beyond that, has resulted in a published work—a dream come true!

With so many people involved right up to the day the books are printed, I am sure I have overlooked someone who rightly deserves to be listed here. Please know this is an oversight. My gratitude goes to you as well!

I could not have finished this project without my husband, Phil. His love, support, encouragement, and belief in me have been amazing. More than once, I have been overwhelmed with the amount of work needed to complete this series. Each time, Phil has reminded me of who I am, whose I am, and the real author and finisher of this work. I love you!!

Finally and most importantly, thank you, God! You have shown me incredible grace and mercy, gifted me in ways I never would have guessed, been gentle in Your rebukes, and showered me with Your blessings. Praise be to You, God our Father and our Lord Jesus Christ!

My gratitude goes out to everyone who has helped and encouraged me ready this manuscript for publication.

Made in the USA
Monee, IL
23 February 2022